REMOTELY EXCEPTIONAL

REMOTELY EXCEPTIONAL

A PLAYBOOK FOR COMPANIES AND THEIR REMOTE WORKERS

KELSEY YUREK

NEW DEGREE PRESS

REMOTELY EXCEPTIONAL

A Playbook for Companies and their Remote Workers

ISBN   978-1-64137-230-5   *Paperback*

            978-1-64137-231-2   *Ebook*

To James and Nancy Yurek, who slingshotted me into the world with the knowledge that you can always make what you want work from anywhere.

CONTENTS

INTRODUCTION

———

In the summer leading up to my senior year at Georgetown, my older brother texted me a CNBC article titled
"How to Make Six Figures on Fiverr," one that I didn't even
open immediately. It's the kind of article that I'd read if
I had time while waiting in my car, standing in line at
the grocery store, or sitting in front of the TV scrolling
on my phone—it didn't immediately grab my attention
or seem relevant to my life. Yet, I found myself sitting
at work, taking one of those all too typical social media
breaks in my cubicle. I came across the following quote
and something seemed to click:

*Being able to set her own hours and schedule, Fasulo says, has
"totally revolutionized her life." As an avid traveler, she can
globe-trot as much as she wants (recent trips include Mexico*

and California), not having to abide by a 9-to-5 schedule or work from an office.[1]

I then knew immediately why my brother had sent it to me. That summer, I had returned home from studying abroad at King's College London, where the culture of academics resulted in far fewer classroom hours than I was accustomed. Naturally, I didn't get any less busy, but I filled my time in different ways. I found myself doing all my academic work on the road as trains, buses, and planes became my library. I studied and wrote in hostels, airports, and train stations. I tasted coffee from around the world just to earn my time on free Wi-Fi. I felt empowered and productive as I did this, and then quickly became uninspired as I returned home to a 9-to-5 internship.

The 9-to-5 routine (at that point) seemed to be a standard for all the "good jobs," and it couldn't have been further from what I wanted. "I just don't feel productive," I often found myself thinking, "I feel useless."

I spent all day with maybe two productive hours in that cubicle, and during all the others I found myself trying to "look busy." And I didn't think I was the only one in my office

---

1   Berger, Sarah. "How this 25-year-old freelancer made $150,000 in 6 months off Fiverr." CNBC. https://www.cnbc.com/2018/06/28/how-to-make-six-figures-on-fiverr.html (June 17, 2019).

doing that. The article started to make the wheels turn in my head.

Flash forward a few months to September of my senior year, and I was still thinking about remote work, particularly this Fiverr article. Fiverr is an online marketplace for freelancers. It's a classic "side hustle" model and is designed for individuals putting up services that start at $5 (more on this later). You didn't need any special qualifications to start. You just needed to be able to sell yourself, which is exactly why it was the perfect way to see if working remotely was all it's cracked up to be.

I was sitting in class, evidently not paying attention (sorry Mom and Dad) and decided it might be worth a shot. I put up a profile for writing blog posts, editing, and proofreading, and then I forgot about it. Based on the little research I had done, it could take a while for new sellers to get started on a freelance platform without intense promotion, so my hopes weren't high.

Four days later, I got a hit on my account. Someone had ordered a service, and it quickly snowballed from there. I received more orders, raised prices to counter demand, and worked to balance my personal (and still very college-oriented) life with this new work style. In fact, I'm still working on it as my account brings in the equivalent of a "real world" salary.

Since then, I've experienced equal parts of "running a business" and working remotely from places like my car, the dentist's office, my parent's couch, a dining room table, a university library, the airport, a coffee shop, and an NBA basketball game. Who says that can't continue to work for other people too? My Fiverr experience is only a small and continual case study of how working remotely operates for large-scale companies out there. As I've talked to remote workers in top industries across the United States, I've learned from their "dos and don'ts" and integrated their suggestions into my own life. And, if I've learned one thing, it's that working remotely has come to benefit my personal and professional world and cause my productivity to skyrocket, and there are very few work arrangements out there that I can say that about.

The statistics out there make a strong case that suggests I'm not the only one who is benefitting from this shift toward remote work. According to Remote.co, **82 percent of remote workers reported lower stress levels** and **80 percent reported higher morale. One in three** workers said that working remotely allowed them to **accomplish more in less time,** and **one in four** said they were able to **accomplish more in the same amount of time.** Furthermore, **68 percent of millennials said that working remotely** was a benefit that increased their interest in any given employer.[2]

---

2   Bibby, Adrianne. "17 Facts About Remote Work in 2019." Remote.co. https://remote.co/10-stats-about-remote-work/ (June 17, 2019).

The more I read about working remotely, the more I saw the benefits for workers—particularly young workers—and I couldn't help but ask myself why this resource wasn't utilized more commonly in the workplace. With $1.8 trillion lost in productivity each year due to chronic health problems, hangovers, stress over childcare, and more, it was time to take a second look at solutions that arise from an unconventional work environment.

This style wasn't new, but it was underutilized, and the more I tried to balance my life as I freelanced remotely, the more I realized that most of us—young and old alike—have never been trained, taught, or prepared to work independently and remotely. It's not that we can't, it's just that we were without data and research on *how* to thrive at remote work.

This book looks at these four core principles for being a successful remote worker in your twenties and thirties. It's a shared responsibility, and it doesn't work unless (a) the employer, (b) the employee, and (c) their direct manager are all on the same page.

- **Building your remote workspace**: While the perception of remote workers involves them working in their PJs from an unmade bed, the reality is that the top remote workers have a clear approach to their remote workspace.

- **Learning how to manage and be managed remotely:** Working remotely doesn't necessarily mean more freedom—it can sometimes mean less freedom, so how you manage and how you are managed is important. Can you master concepts like asynchronous communication, work-life balance when you're always at home and always at the office, and being effective for your team when you're not with them?

- **Facilitating blended work:** One of the biggest concerns among remote workers is a feeling of loneliness, which has led many companies to look toward creating a blended work approach with some remote and some in-office work structures.

- **Finding remote work:** As a younger worker, how do you combat the stigma of wanting to work remotely because you are not "ambitious?" Where do you look for these remote work options?

The book takes a look at this from two perspectives: (a) working remotely as a twenty-something or thirty-something employee, and (b) hiring and managing remote workers in their twenties and thirties.

Working remotely isn't for everyone. It isn't something you can force in an office culture (as Yahoo proved in 2013). Yet, it is something that benefits those who need it as a resource to increase their productivity, and it can help attract top talent who can and should be able to work anywhere in the world. This book is for anyone who sees a need for change in their situation—whether you're an employee or an employer—from the idea that working remotely is only for the exceptional.

With the right mindset, remote work can be a one-size-fits-all solution to many of the office problems workers experience today. It eliminates distractions and family challenges while creating options for those who dislike the 9-to-5 routine, allowing for more flexibility overall. Together, employees and employers can work together to create a beneficial arrangement for both parties that keeps both productivity and collaboration up in an atypical work environment. Where it serves employee and employer, remote work is in, and desk jobs are out.

PART 1

WORKING REMOTELY

CHAPTER 1

HOW WE GOT HERE

———

For a few years in the early 2000s, my dad worked remotely from a home office. Of course, at the time, the only thing this meant for me was that I had to be fairly quiet when I got home from half-day kindergarten because "Dad was on a conference call." Inconvenient, right?

I had no idea what it meant then to work remotely. During his work day—when he wasn't traveling or visiting store locations because he works in sales—he'd connect with his team using tools that were just beginning to emerge: cell phones, laptops, and wireless internet. None of those were truly relevant in a home office before then.

These memories continue to bring me back to an underlying theme that I reflected on as I've researched and interviewed remote workers today. Remote work isn't new, but it is underutilized. In fact, when you pose the questions, "Where did this all start? How did we get here?" you don't have to look far from your own home. Most will say that "working from home" started in hunter-gatherer times and progressed throughout history as artisans made use of the space they had at home for their trade. Today, where we are is largely a product of where we've been.

THE MODERN OFFICE IN HISTORY

As merchants and craftspeople were the first true "home-workers" with their shops situated within their living quarters, the development of the modern office is an interesting revolution. The Industrial Revolution is the turning point of what pulled workers from the home and into factories that had hours set by employers. Despite the fact that we now have technology that makes such a work environment unnecessary and outdated (unless it serves the worker), it is the widely accepted model.

From factories, the modern office continued to improve into the twentieth century.[3] When you look at early technology like electricity, typewriters, telegraphs, and telephones, these

---

3   Reynolds, Brie Weiler. "The Complete History of Working from Home." Flex Jobs. https://www.flexjobs.com/blog/post/complete-history-of-working-from-home/ (June 17, 2019).

were the baby steps that allows workers to have offices that functioned well.[4] Women were welcomed into the workplace as typewriters and telephones meant that they could have "pink collar" jobs as secretaries.[5]

The 1970s saw the push toward telecommuting as we see it today. The movement was spearheaded by Jack Nilles, a former NASA engineer who wrote the 1973 book *The Telecommunications-Transportation Tradeoff.*[6] While the book primarily focused on reducing the amount of traffic and pollution caused by workers traveling to and from the office, it set the framework for what remote work could look like.[7]

Since then, remote work has slowly crept into the workplace with companies in large cities—like New York City and Chicago—implementing it first. Technology has transformed the ways that remote workers can be integrated into the workplace and the ways in which communication can occur.

---

4   Ibid.
5   Ibid.
6   Greenfield, Rebecca. "Telecommuting." Bloomberg. https://www. bloomberg.com/quicktake/telecommuting (June 17, 2019).
7   Ibid.

HOW TECHNOLOGY CHANGED WORKING REMOTELY

Just as the remote work revolution began and Nilles began to spearhead the prospect of working remotely as a solution to a number of different issues, technology began to emerge that would help supplement the future of work. WeWork, one of the top coworking spaces for remote workers today, documents just how central technology has been in improving remote work in its history in the timeline.

In **1975**, the first "personal" computer was released. While this computer still came years before the MacBooks and Lenovos that keep us connected now, it was a vital step in what would one day become a tool that made remote work accessible to all.[8]

In **1990**, the World Wide Web was invented, making the internet both mainstream and accessible. This was the beginning of email and virtual office tools that workplaces across the world could use to connect and create. In this same year, the government also conducted a remote work study that highlighted the benefits for two thousand federal workers. An increase in productivity, improved work-life balance, and a reduction in expenses and commuting time were observed.[9]

---

8   "The History, Evolution and Future of Remote Work." WeWork. https://weworkremotely.com/history-of-remote-work (June 17, 2019).

9   Ibid.

In **1994** and **1995**, big companies like American Express and IBM were the first to begin to allow employees to work remotely.[10]

In **1997**, Google was first launched as a search engine. Today, it forms the foundation for a variety of tools necessary in a remote work setting. Gmail, GChat, Google Hangouts, Google Calendar, and Google Drive are among some of the most predominant tools.[11]

In the **early 2000s**, the internet became wireless, allowing remote workers to truly become remote. Rather than relying purely on a home office to be able to connect to the internet using an Ethernet cable, Wi-Fi revolutionized how work could be done. Digital nomads were born, coworking spaces were created, and travel became possible.[12]

In **2002** and **2003**, two still-predominant tools that connected workers were launched. LinkedIn allowed old friends and coworkers to connect in a virtual sphere, and companies could now advertise job opportunities without ever making physical contact with their potential employees. The next year, Skype was launched, a communication tool that could better serve remote workers by helping maintain the

---

10   Ibid.
11   Ibid.
12   Ibid.

face-to-face connection that's valued in the workplace as well as in remote interviews.[13]

In **2009**, Slack created an internal channel for workplaces everywhere. It has since become the fastest-growing business application in history with eight million active daily users. For many remote teams, Slack is the quickest and most effective way to communicate.[14]

In **2012**, Google Drive was added to Google's suite of office tools, making it easier for remote workers to upload and access all necessary documents from anywhere in the world. Working in real time is now easier than ever when a person in Hong Kong, a person in the United Kingdom, and a person in New York can all access and edit the same document simultaneously.[15]

In **2016**, Dell reported that expansion of their remote work program resulted in savings of over $12 million...*annually.* While remote work provides incredible opportunities for workers to increase productivity and seek better work-life balance, companies are finding that it has hidden benefits for them as well—many of which are financial.[16]

---

13   Ibid.
14   Ibid.
15   "The History, Evolution and Future of Remote Work." WeWork. https://weworkremotely.com/history-of-remote-work (June 17, 2019).
16   Ibid.

In **2017**, cities like San Francisco and Austin reported that between 30 to 60 percent (respectively) of their jobs went to remote workers. When remote work is in play, a zip code doesn't have to be a limiting factor in accessing top talent.[17]

REMOTE WORK TODAY

Remote work is not without critics and naysayers who preach that the way to get anything done is to sit in the office. Yet, the statistics and the rise of remote work throughout history say otherwise.

Remote work (among the non-self-employed) has grown immensely in the last fifteen years. Since 2005, it has grown by nearly 140 percent, which means it's growing nearly ten times faster than the rest of the workforce.[18] Around 4.3 million people currently work remotely, which means 4.3 million people out there are reaping these flexible benefits.[19]

With the proper support and tools, there's nothing stopping the remote workforce. Now the only thing to ask is...could you be joining it?

---

17   Ibid.
18   Hernandez, Brigeda. "21 Statistics About Remote Work Trends in 2018." Skip the Drive. https://www.skipthedrive.com/21-statistics-about-remote-work-trends-in-2018/ (June 17, 2019).
19   "The History, Evolution and Future of Remote Work." WeWork. https://weworkremotely.com/history-of-remote-work (June 17, 2019).

CHAPTER 2

IS REMOTE WORK FOR YOU?

————

The decision to work remotely might come with a little hesitation if you've never done it before. After all, if you've always thought that you'd graduate high school, go to college, and work at an office building, it's certainly a change in perspective. Yet, today **83 percent of workers do not feel that they need an office to be productive.**[20] Changing your workspace could improve your productivity, even if you've never done it before.

20 Hernandez, Brigeda. "21 Statistics About Remote Work Trends in 2018." Skip the Drive. https://www.skipthedrive.com/21-statistics-about-remote-work-trends-in-2018/ (June 17, 2019).

To make it easier to comprehend this change, this chapter includes a short quiz that can help you determine whether or not working remotely is the right choice for you. The statements below aren't the be-all and end-all in choosing whether working remotely is the right step, but they can help direct your steps if you're considering it.

Working remotely requires that you partner with your employer and direct manager and also understand your own work style. Naturally, this means that remote work isn't for everyone. Some individuals feel that they can't be productive in an unstructured environment, and that's okay too! What's important is that you're seeking productivity, which makes you a better worker. If that means you start your work day at 6 a.m. and finish it at 2 p.m., maybe that's just your style. If it means you work in two-hour spurts with the ability to go to the gym, pick up kids, walk the dog, run errands, or travel, that might also be the case as long as you're being productive.

Take this quiz to see if working remotely might be a better fit for your lifestyle and productivity:

- You can stay motivated and organized on your own timeline
- You're a self-starter and don't rely on intense collaboration with others (i.e. stopping by someone's desk to throw ideas around) in order to begin a project

- You ideal "day in the office" doesn't align with a typical 9-to-5 routine
- Your lifestyle (kids, health, dogs, travel, commute) would benefit from having increased flexibility with your hours
- You find your work environment and coworkers distracting because of noise or constant interruptions
- You are a confident communicator and feel you can communicate effectively via email, instant messaging, text, phone calls, video conferencing, or other messaging platforms rather than by in-person conversations
- You have a job where you have tangible deliverables that can demonstrate progress remotely
- Your role isn't a "forward-facing" role. While you have a vital role in helping your company, you're not the person who is face-to-face with a customer every single day (i.e. nursing)
- You have a space that you can dedicate to productive work
- You have a job where you understand the policies and procedures well enough to do them remotely and without the direct assistance of a supervisor
- You do not struggle with feeling lonely if you are not constantly around a community of people
- You have the ability to create a healthy work-life balance while working remotely (consider all factors involved: whether you're single, in a relationship, married, have kids, etc.)

You don't have to meet all of the above criteria to work remotely, but some jobs simply aren't a good fit. For example, if you work in retail or nursing, you won't be working remotely because your roles are forward-facing for the company. Consumers see your face every single day, which means not being present in the workplace simply doesn't make sense.

That said, other roles (and there are many of them out there!) align perfectly with a remote work framework. Think jobs in technology, jobs in human resources, jobs in insurance, jobs in healthcare, jobs in management, jobs in business, jobs in financial sectors, and more. While there are some that definitely can't fit into the mold, there are an endless number of jobs that can.

If you're looking to make this jump and you're a good fit so far, keep reading! There's much ahead from both perspectives in terms of how you can be an effective remote worker and how you can make your professional environment work for you. Now is the time to learn how you can seamlessly pitch remote work to your employer!

CHAPTER 3

HOW TO MAKE YOUR PROFESSIONAL ENVIRONMENT WORK FOR YOU

———

YOU ARE VALUABLE TO THE COMPANY.

Over the past year, I've interviewed dozens and dozens of successful remote workers. The most common thing they had in common was confidence that they were valuable to their employers.

Time and time again, conversations with remote workers made it clear how much *more* valuable they found themselves to their company when they developed a work style that aligned to their own aims and desires.

And on the other side, people who wished they could work remotely all seemed to believe that if they asked their employer or pushed harder on the idea of remote work, they'd be turned down, or worse, replaced.

If you want to enjoy your work (remote or not), YOU have to design your work style. And one piece of that is deciding how remote work should fit into that style.

* * *

Anya Sanger spent fifteen years with Prosperity Life Insurance Group and those fifteen years involved an hour-long commute in and out of Manhattan from her New Jersey home. Eventually, the summer of 2017 rolled around, and Sanger had had it. She wanted to move back up to Massachusetts to spend more time with her family. While she spent some time looking for jobs, she also wanted to see if there was an opportunity for her to take her job with her and work remotely.

Sanger first approached her boss, who actually worked remotely out of Chicago himself. She let him know that she was going to be relocating, that she didn't want to leave her position, and that she hoped they could work something out. Her boss, a remote worker himself, didn't seem to have any concerns at all. The problem stemmed from Sanger's position within the company.

"The CEO was not on board with remote working in general," Sanger remembered.

Yet, while her CEO didn't love the idea, people at her company still did it, and they were willing to work with Sanger on a contract basis. She just couldn't keep her position. As a high-level manager, Sanger wasn't able to take that role remotely. So, Prosperity Life created a new position that she could make a remote role.

Sanger notes that her work remained largely the same outside of the fact that she didn't have a formal leadership role anymore. In the first few months, she continued to transition any projects that couldn't be performed remotely to the individual who took over her role on the floor of the New York office.

Initially, Sanger was only supposed to have a three to six-month remote contract with Prosperity Life. But after that first period, it got extended...and then again once more after that. When she didn't receive a third renewal, Sanger noted it was "probably a cost savings thing." She didn't receive any indication that there was a performance reason they didn't renew her contract.

In fact, Sanger said, "If anything, I was putting in way more time."

* * *

Engagement is a world-wide issue for companies. How do you keep workers not only productive and active at your company, but happy as well? A 2017 NBC News article highlights how research shows employers mistakenly conflating salary raises and employee happiness in the workplace.[21] Rather than seeing potential benefits like increasing employee autonomy, which often results in higher productivity and morale, employers tend to "throw money at the problem."[22]

What type of autonomy are we talking about? The ability to make decisions, contribute ideas, work with limited supervision, determine responsibilities, and more. In essence, employees want the ability to work without being micromanaged, and they want to be able to determine some of their own responsibilities. This autonomy allows them to

---

21 Demers, Jayson. "Research says this is the secret to being happy at work." NBC News. https://www.nbcnews.com/better/careers/research-says-secret-being-happy-work-n762926 (June 17, 2019).

22 Ibid.

thrive in their productivity and in their position, which only benefits the company.

It's important to note that remote work is just one part of autonomy—it's a big one for the purposes of this book—but it's critical to know that the first step in the journey is creating autonomy in your career and success in your role.

* * *

As LinkedIn has emerged as the premier social networking site for business professionals, it's launched new ways to attract traffic and increase its own credibility. Its weekly emails to users now include articles of interest, and one caught my attention during my months of researching remote work. It was called "Why the Eight-Hour Work Day Doesn't Work." Simple, catchy, and my first thought? "Well, duh."

The article highlights a computer study conducted by the Draugiem Group that uses a computer application to track work habits. The major finding confirmed what I've known to be true based on my own work habits and what nearly every remote worker I conversed with has indicated: The length of their workday was ultimately insignificant.

Yet, the way that their workday was structured was crucial in creating productivity. Working long hours doesn't make you productive. It actually makes you more prone to taking a "Facebook break" or to work more slowly because of fatigue. Those who were better at working in 50-minute spurts with short refreshers were able to get their work done more quickly in a shorter amount of time.

So, how does working remotely fit into all of this? The better question is, how does it not? If an eight-hour work day doesn't result in productivity, then the 9-to-5 office model is irrelevant *unless* it serves the employee. When considering remote work for yourself or your workplace, your first question should be...

How can I make my professional environment work for me?

Anya Sanger initially received pushback but realized her own happiness was critical to be more productive at work.

With the switch to remote work, Sanger was actually dedicating more time to her responsibilities. But at the same time, her productivity was also much higher. The number of distractions in an office, especially for Sanger, who has ADHD, presents a real challenge to her productivity. She said she found herself being more productive and putting in more hours because she was "trying to prove herself" in her remote role.

Sanger attributes the CEO's reluctance toward remote work to a generational divide in the workplace: "Older people want to see you at the office early, at your desk a lot, and leaving the office late," she said.

The problem with that? "Just because you're there doesn't mean you're actually working. When you're working remotely there's a challenge to prove yourself, and I think that's why people are more productive."

Outside of increased work productivity, how else did Sanger's life change as a result of remote work? After all, it all started because she wanted to spend more time with her family. Sanger said she got back three hours each day because she wasn't commuting, and she loved it.

"It was so life changing. I could pick up my son from school and see him more when he got home. It made such a difference in the amount of time I had."

Sanger also saved money on new work clothes, commuting, eating out, and small expenses like coffee.

Now that her time with Prosperity Life is over, Sanger says she's actively seeking out remote work opportunities. Her only reservation is being able to grow and develop as a manager at a new company while also working remotely. She acknowledges visibility is lower and it may be challenging to excel without knowing people first.

Nonetheless, her nine months as a remote worker has her convinced "it's a benefit for the employees" regardless of generational differences in thought at the workplace.

* * *

Sanger's experience isn't an isolated one. Erin Landis experienced it as well. It drove her from the office and right into starting her own business.

The first six of Landis' fifteen years in property management were at a property management firm, but she's since moved to being her own boss. Landis' company was born out of a variety of factors: generational differences in work environments, inflexible work arrangements while she was pregnant and after giving birth, and most of all just seeing the increase in efficiency that remote work enabled in an industry that used to be solely brick-and-mortar.

"Looking back I realize there was only one person who really 'got it,'" she says of her experience in her firm's office.

Despite the fact that her industry didn't typically accommodate remote work, Landis said it often made more sense from 2005-9 to work remotely, at least occasionally, due to distractions: "The office I worked in was loud (phones constantly ringing, people talking over the intercom), and mostly filled with people who were clueless."

Prior to 2009, GoToMyPC, a remote work desktop software that allows individuals to access computers remotely via web browser, and similar programs were the most common in her industry. After 2009, Landis says the shift to web-based software in the property management industry made a significant difference. "Once I got us migrated to the new system, we also switched email to go through Gmail. This made working from anywhere a viable option. I'd sometimes work from home two to three days out of the week," she says.

Not only did this make work easier on her, it also increased her efficiency. Her work was getting done faster, and she didn't have to worry about the constant interruptions in the office space. Yet, Landis was up against a generational divide in thinking at work—not everyone agreed that it was the best practice.

"There were always those in the office—all baby boomer aged—who acted like I was totally unavailable, even though I was in my email and available via chat all day long," she remembers.

It began to shift when Landis got pregnant and her boss knew that a lack of flexibility could impact her ability to continue to work. "My boss, the owner of the company, told me 'Whatever you need to do to make this work, feel free, we don't want to lose you,'"Landis said.

That's when Landis began to consistently work remotely for three days of the week to get everyone in her office used to the dynamic before her baby arrived. Yet, despite the flexibility her boss originally conveyed, the process became increasingly less flexible as Landis' pregnancy progressed.

"It was fine until I was put on bed rest at thirty-four weeks for crazy high blood pressure and couldn't drive. My calendar was shared with my boss, so she knew when I'd be at the doctor and not available," she said. However, at one doctor's appointment, Landis received an email from her boss. The email asked when she was coming back, specified that she had to be back within six weeks of her daughter being born, and restricted her ability to work remotely for the rest of the year.

"I would only be able to work from home two days of the week through the end of the year (this was in August), then I'd need to be in the office every day," she said.

The stress of trying to make her work arrangement work, in addition to the high blood pressure her pregnancy had induced, led to preeclampsia, a potentially dangerous medical complication that can occur during pregnancy. Landis was induced at 36 weeks with no childcare lined up.

Although her boss had originally been lenient with Landis and her remote work arrangement, she retracted her original commitment. Why? "Her justification for going back on what she'd agreed to was, 'When the rubber meets the road, it just won't work, everyone needs you here every day.'"

So, Landis never went back. She wasn't making enough to justify paying for childcare, and she didn't understand the mentality of the baby boomers in her office. "They liked people sitting there to take phone calls, which is not really necessary if you train people or you make it easy for people to contact you every other way on earth," she said.

When her daughter was a few months old, Landis was approached by someone to start a property management company. It took almost a year to get it up and running, but once it did, it operated almost entirely remotely except for a tiny room they used for an office suite. They accepted payments in person (although online payments were strongly encouraged), showed properties, and met people to sign leases and give keys.

That company didn't last forever due to some management issues, but Landis and one of her partners started over one last time. They were both determined to make it work this time and to do everything as efficiently as possible.

"Property management, before everything became web-based, was dependent on having an office to get keys, sign leases, accept payments. Once everything changed it made sense to sign leases online, take online payments, take maintenance requests online. Doing so eliminated lots of inefficiencies and wasted time," she says.

So, that's what they did. She and her partner never had an office. In Texas, where she lives, property management agents can utilize a walk-in postal center as their "office." Landis and her partner took a high-touch industry and made it low-touch. "We use self-showing lock boxes for showings, all our applications are accepted online, leases are sent and signed electronically, and all payments are made online," she says.

In general, Landis finds that the property management business used to be for an older generation up until the last few years. "Renters have become more tech-savvy and expect the same of us. It's a tough business, lots of people hate their property managers, but it has nothing to do with where we do business," Landis said.

The way Landis and her partner operate their business is admittedly "a bit of an anomaly," she said. The brick-and-mortar property management business sees this approach as cold and disconnected because it often cuts out in-person communication. She says, "People say, 'How can you move a tenant in and have never seen them in person before?'"

Yet, Landis knows they're connecting with people, particularly young people, in a way that they prefer to operate anyway. They personally communicate with everyone and verify everything. Their communication is mostly via site chat and texting, and it's proven to create a good rapport with current tenants. Phone calls are not a millennial's favorite method of communication, and Landis' business model caters directly to that.

She believes that there are additional benefits from the consumer side of operating remotely. Since Landis and her partner know nothing about the applicants except their income, housing history, etc., they avoid many of the issues that come with fair housing laws. Gender, race, ethnicity, and other social identifiers are not part of their application process. The first time they see the individual who is renting property is when the tenant submits a selfie on the property itself to receive the code for the lock box. "We all operate with bias whether or not we intend to," Landis recognized. She believes this is one way to eliminate the risk of it in her daily business.

Landis also acknowledges the personal benefits that remote work provides to both her and her business partner: "We're available to be there for our kids' school parties, days off, and sick days without thinking twice."

They've also continued to maintain these personal and business benefits through the use of a virtual assistant. "We were outsourcing a few tasks to a virtual assistant company, but we found working with a pool of virtual assistants to be inefficient so we hired a full-time, dedicated virtual assistant after a brief experience having a local assistant who wasn't getting anything done."

So, not only has their business provided Landis and her partner with the ability to work remotely, but it's also providing the same ability to a young woman across the world. We'll call her Megan. Megan currently lives in the Philippines where, according to Landis, "it's become really popular for people to work overnight" because of the amount of money that can be made.

Megan is currently married with a five-year-old and attending law school. Landis and her partner recently shifted Megan's hours to 1-9 CT at her request and found it helped their business more than they expected. "We quickly realized it was good for us as it allows us to have someone available after 5 when more people are off work and handling personal business," Landis said.

Landis describes Megan's work ethic as unlike any other employee they worked with in the United States. "She's a vital part of our team who we genuinely care about the same as if she were here," Landis explained. "For her, this is a dream job as she's making more than she'd make anywhere else and she's at home with her son."

To communicate, the three have regular Skype calls and chat with her via Google Hangouts frequently throughout the day. Landis says Megan's online a full eight hours "monitoring everything she needs to, responding to inquiries, solving problems that arise."

Overall, Landis sees a remote virtual assistant as an opportunity to impact a young family in a global economy. Megan's been their "best decision ever." And they aren't the only ones taking this route. Plenty of individuals either go through a third-party company to pay virtual assistants across the world or simply PayPal their income to them.

Landis spoke so much about the benefits that I began to wonder if there was anything out there that was more difficult for a property management company operating as a rarity in the industry, without a brick-and-mortar front. "No," she says, "It's so much better to me that when people talk about needing to have an office, I don't get it."

Her path to remote work was bumpy, but it ended with the creation of her company. Landis couldn't be more pleased with her situation. She enjoys the benefits she lacked in her previous property management position of setting hours, having flexibility with now two children, and working with coworkers who operate similarly—one of whom is across the world. Landis didn't let the fact that her office couldn't accommodate remote work stop her, and she didn't let the fact that property management was historically brick-and-mortar deter her either. Landis' persistence in finding what worked for her and her ability to adjust business elements to allow her virtual assistant more flexibility—a decision that ended up benefiting the company overall—demonstrate key traits of successful remote workers and designate Landis as a trailblazer in her industry.

* * *

Laura Meier-Schmitz is a final, "real-life" example of an individual who saw how her employment situation could improve from remote work and didn't hesitate to move forward. Back in 2013, she discovered through necessity that she was the "perfect" remote work candidate at her seventy-person CPA firm, and it has changed her life ever since.

When her daughter was born, Meier-Schmitz opted to breast-feed but found that once she went back to work, it was too hard to pump. "Offices aren't set up for privacy like that," she said.

Her office wasn't massive, but it was sizable enough that seeing people day-to-day was considered essential. Generally, people weren't allowed to work remotely. However, her work was much more isolated. This made her an ideal candidate, so she decided to ask the managing partner if she could work from home to help mitigate the problem she was having.

"He agreed immediately, and I started to work from home two times a week," Meier-Schmitz said.

Slowly, she started to work remotely more and more until she was at home about 80 percent of the time. She had a second child and went through maternity leave. Meier-Schmitz eventually returned to the company, but it just wasn't working, so she left to start her own business in April 2017.

Today, Meier-Schmitz has built up enough clients in her small bookkeeping business that she's hoping to bring some of her own employees on board this spring. Her positive experience with remote work has influenced the way she hopes to run her company after the initial onboarding process.

"When I hire my first employee, it is my intention to rent a work share space to do the training and progress to them working remotely."

However, Meier-Schmitz is still open to maintaining a physical workspace if individuals would like somewhere more formal than a home environment: "I'll book WeWork spaces for a couple months to work together to get them trained and then I would be happy to keep that space and extend it if they wanted it."

While working remotely was initially a solution related to her new motherhood responsibilities, Meier-Schmitz has a clear boundary between her work and her parenting. Working remotely made pumping significantly easier, but she doesn't have her kids at home with her while she works.

"I don't consider myself billable to a client if I'm taking care of a child because my work takes all of my focus," she says.

Despite the fact that kids made working in an office setting tough, working from home in general just meant that she had a lot more time.

"It was really tough with an eight-hour work day, thirty minutes for lunch, and an hour commute each way," she remembered, "Not to mention the standards of appearance for working at home are a lot lower."

Living in Minnesota, the weather was a huge factor in morning routines (shoveling and scraping) and morning commute times (traffic). The overall efficiency that remote work offered to Meier-Schmitz was unmatchable. After seeing the impact it had on her life and career, she became a small business owner instead of opting to go back into a large company.

So the real question is, would she ever go back?

To that, she says, "I'm pretty happy with this. It would depend on how big my team ever got and if I ever had a need for a more organized meeting space." For now, she's content where she is, building up her business in the comfort of her own home.

* * *

These three stories are only a few of the thousands out there in which remote workers have altered their work environments out of necessity. Remote work isn't about saving your company money—although that is a convenient byproduct—it's about bringing value to your company. Are you doing that now? How could you be doing it better with increased autonomy in your workplace and your workspace?

PART 2

THRIVING REMOTELY

CHAPTER 4

BUILD YOUR REMOTE WORKSPACE

———

While the stereotype is that remote workers lounge around in their pajama pants, the reality is that a remote workspace is something that each individual remote employee builds in order to maximize their productivity. It can be anything from a home office to a coffee shop to a co-working space down the street or around the world. As remote workers break down the need to go into a traditional office setting each and every day, new knowledge and research on how to create a remote workspace that promotes success emerges. Remote.co names five core elements that are necessary in a remote work setting: connectivity, physical comfort, privacy, noise level, and access to amenities.[23] Throughout this chapter, each of these elements will be discussed as helpful mechanisms for remote workers in building their optimal workspace.

* * *

Greg Caplan is the CEO and co-founder of a start-up that caters directly to remote workers who want to travel while they work, but he never initially intended to start a company. This start-up, Remote Year, is a platform that allows individuals who work remotely to travel in a community. Remote Year currently has a four-month and twelve-month experience where the program visits four places and twelve places respectively. In an August 2018 episode of *Nomad Podcast*, he explains how he built a platform that now takes digital nomads around the globe when all he originally intended to do was travel the world himself.[24]

"For me, it started from day one about it being all about community," he said.

Caplan's strong sense of community comes from his personal background. He grew up in the suburbs of Chicago

---

23 Depaul, Kristi. "5 Things to Look for in a Remote Workspace." Remote.co. https://remote.co/things-look-for-remote-workspace/ (June 17, 2019).

24 Tierney, Sean. "Ep 9: Greg Caplan of Remote Year." *Nomad Podcast*. https://nomad-podcast.com/greg-caplan-remote-year/ (June 17, 2019).

in what he calls a "fairly cookie cutter upbringing from US standards." Yet, he credits his global awareness from a young age to his parents.

"When I was five, my parents met this guy, Salin Butler. He was a Kiwi from New Zealand in his early 20s and needed a place to stay for a couple weeks," Caplan remembers, "They invited him to stay with us for a couple weeks, and we really hit it off, so a couple weeks actually turned into over five years, and he became like a brother to me."

The incredible experience that the Caplan family had from bringing Butler into their home and learning from him prompted them to continue more of these experiences. Over the next several years, they continued to welcome others into their home—individuals from places like South Africa, Australia, North Africa, and Russia. Caplan said that this "mini-Model UN around the dinner table every night in our little cul-de-sac in suburbia" really opened his mind up to global perspectives. He said it also, more importantly, created "a really strong mark on me around community, so I just love being with big groups of people all the time, and so whenever I do anything, I don't really care what I'm doing, but I care who I'm doing it with and making sure I'm with a big group of people."

This mindset became instrumental in looking at how Caplan initially founded Remote Year. At the time, he was working at

Groupon in a traditional work environment. It was a 9-to-5 job with an open office environment, and he says he just felt "stuck." The work style and work pattern weren't working for him, so Caplan came up with a new idea. He went out and found a remote work opportunity. He thought that he could feel "unstuck" by traveling and seeing the world. But for him, he needed to do that in a community.

He said, "Again, whenever I do anything, I start with 'who.' So at dinner one night, I asked my group of best friends, 'Do you guys want to get remote jobs and go travel together?' And they all kind of looked at me like I was crazy and said, 'What are you talking about? That doesn't make any sense at all.' So basically, the next day I put up a website. 'Who wants to travel together for a year while working remotely. If you do, put your email address in here.' When my intention was really to just find a group of people to travel with for a while."

While that may have been Caplan's intention, that's not exactly how it transpired. Caplan sent it to what he calls a "couple of friends" who he thought might know some people who would be interested in this type of work-travel experience. Those friends sent it to more friends who sent it to more friends. That chain ended up amassing over a thousand sign-ups in the first day. Over the next few months, the posting that Caplan had created actually got picked up in newspaper publications worldwide.

"Before I knew it 50,000 people signed up so there's really strong interest, really a lot of excitement, you know. Looking back, I think there's some macro trends that propelled that." Caplan said, "But, you know, during that period of time when all these people are signing up for what's basically a scammy-looking website of just like an email sign-up box, that's when, you know, I was talking to my roommate at the time and said there's something bigger here than just finding a group of friends to travel with. Let's try to formalize this into something a little bit more structured. And that's really where the idea of Remote Year turned into more of an organization than just a ragtag group of friends kind of experiencing the world together."

Yet, Remote Year didn't become an organization overnight. In the next few months, Caplan spent a lot of time figuring out the logistics. What started out as a theoretical idea on the internet grew into a real program in June 2015. In just six months, the first group of "remotes" showed up in Prague, Czech Republic. Though, even then, Caplan didn't know that it would continue to grow beyond what it was then. He didn't think too much about it. Remember, this all started because Caplan just wanted to do something different with his own work environment.

"Early on, it was clear that there was this groundswell of interest and excitement for what we were doing, so I didn't sort of think too much then of what it could be or how it could evolve," Caplan says, "But honestly, from day one, like this notion of, you know, working flexibly and experiencing the world struck a chord with lots of people. So, I definitely understood that there were big possibilities for what this thing could become but it's humbling every day to see how quickly it's actually unfolded and touched so many lives."

So, exactly how does Remote Year touch so many people's lives? You might be wondering why someone who works remotely already and has this desire to travel the world wouldn't just go and do so on their own. Remote Year caters to exactly a group that has the ability but wouldn't do it by themselves. For the people in this group, it's all about community.

"We bring together an amazing group of people and you share this experience together," Caplan says.

The funny thing about that though is that a lot of the remotes don't realize that's a core reason behind why they join the experience. While a lot of people may initially come for the logistics and global travel experience, they end up loving the benefits of being in a community and the exposure they have to other individuals who are doing exactly what they are doing. With Remote Year, you end up paying a lump sum of money in the beginning and then a monthly fee. For your money, these are the benefits you receive:

- A private, furnished room in each location. This room might be within a shared house or apartment of other Remote Year participants.
- Access to a 24/7 co-working space which is within thirty minutes of your accommodation.
- Educational and cultural activities in your location.
- Transportation by either plane or bus to each of the locations on the itinerary.
- Support. Both to help individuals convince their employers that Remote Year is an enriching experience as well as on the ground support when individuals are in each city.

Caplan says that Remote Year has essentially found that there's a formula for people to have these transformative life experiences that he was seeking when he quit Groupon. This includes a combination of high-quality workspaces, pleasant accommodations, great events and activities, and good travel experiences. Together, this has proven to help remotes grow both professionally and personally. "Ultimately, we want to provide the foundation for folks to have these experiences," Caplan continues, "We're a platform for people to use however they want to."

Remote Year has grown since their initial trip in June 2015 with seventy remotes. They now have two primary types of trips as mentioned in the beginning of this section. There's a four-month experience and a twelve-month experience. However, Caplan says that the creation of these different experiences has largely been to reach individuals who have different needs while also connecting back to Remote Year's mission. He says, "As an organization, we want to try to create lots of different experiences for folks that match what they're looking for [and] that are connected with our mission. And our mission is to make the world a more peaceful and productive place by fostering authentic human connections among diverse people and cultures."

The four-month experience is important because Caplan says some individuals just can't commit to a full twelve months. Understandably, due to professional or personal commitments, a year can be a lengthy amount of time. "So, we created a four-month experience to be a little bit more inclusive of people with different life situations. We'll continue to create new products and experiences to expose people to diverse experiences across the world as much as we possibly can as long as it's on mission and, you know, includes more folks in our experiences," Caplan said.

Diversity and inclusion are a primary mission of Remote Year and it's something they look at heavily while selecting their applicants. In terms of participation, Remote Year has around 60 percent of their participation coming from inside the United States and 40 percent participation as non-US

They look a lot at geographic diversity, but it can be tough with the price being set in US dollars as currencies are constantly devalued. Caplan says they have a large LGBTQ community that joins Remote Year, which is great. He also says they look a lot at the type of culture they create because it isn't just about diversity but also about inclusion and constantly how they could include more of the population in these types of experiences. The diversity and inclusion conversation is tough, and Caplan says they "could always improve" but it is something of which Remote Year is cognizant.

Remote Year may take remote workers around the world, but it doesn't do it arbitrarily. It pays special attention to the accommodations that workers need to be productive on the road. The core elements that go into building your remote workspace are something to be thoughtful about from the get-go.

* * *

Remote workers face challenges when creating a successful workplace. In fact, if a remote worker doesn't build the right kind of workplace outside the office, they may face the same kind of issues that they did while inside the office. Focusing on the five core elements are vital to ensuring that these obstacles don't hinder productivity—after all, your environment should encourage it.

CONNECTIVITY

"The first macro trend is that work is fundamentally changing, right? You see the technology sort of enabling that," Caplan said, "The tools and processes and productivity in the Cloud. You could do great work from anywhere, and communication's digital."

Connectivity is definitional in allowing any remote worker to thrive. In fact, any workspace loses its appeal if you can't get on the Wi-Fi. If you go to a coffee shop to do work and the Wi-Fi is slow, what are the odds that you finish out the work day there? Next to none. Connectivity is vital in ensuring that you can gain access to the documents and databases that you need. It also allows you to work with individuals that you'd be interacting with if you were in an actual office space.

Work is more different than it has ever been before because technology allows it to be. The culture of organizations is shifting because we have tools that allow us to connect with people all over the world, and we can do so almost instantly. Caplan hits on this point exactly.

Working remotely isn't limited to the home anymore because of the tools available to you. He said, "This is now possible based on the tools, but I think culturally more and more organizations are getting comfortable with the idea that you don't need everyone together in one room. And it's actually very difficult and costly and challenging to require everyone to be in the same room in order to be on the same team [now] that this macro trend around work becoming more flexible is happening meaningfully and more and more jobs are able to be done from anywhere."

Caplan even compares the acceptance of remote workers to the acceptance of other functions in the workplace like the Cloud and Slack. These are programs that the workplace really couldn't fathom operating without now, but at the time they were proposed, their adoption cycle was fairly slow. "Slack did a really good job infiltrating specific users and those users shared it across other users," Caplan said. This is exactly how remote work will operate. It will be a "bottom up type of thing" as he calls it, where a few workers start out and then bring more and more coworkers on board.

PHYSICAL COMFORT

Being comfortable in your workspace is a necessity, and it's why we picture remote workers working from their beds in the first place. Because let's be honest, working in your pajamas has some appeal. Yet, creating physical comfort in your workplace doesn't have to mean you spend all day in bed. It's about recognizing what appeals to you in a workspace. Are you more comfortable in spaces with natural or artificial lighting? Do you like to work in a more informal couch setting, or do you need a table or desk set-up to get something done? Do you find you get antsy sitting altogether and would rather stand while working or have the ability to walk around during calls or between bursts of work? Creating your workspace is all about knowing how you can find physical comfort. For some, it can be found in a co-working space or a coffee shop. For others, that kind of comfort is only found at home, which is why the office didn't work out in the first place.

PRIVACY & NOISE LEVEL

One Georgetown alum in the greater Boston Area spent time as a remote worker after reaching a compromise with her former employer, the US Citizenship and Immigration Services (USCIS). For her protection and privacy, she requested that her name not be used, so we'll call her Melissa Johnson.

Johnson relocated to Boston with her boyfriend who was in the military, but she didn't want to give up her role as a management and program analyst at USCIS. She arranged a one-week-on, one-week-off remote work policy that eased the amount of commuting she'd have to do as a temporary solution and found that it really aligned with her preferred style of work.

Her team of nine people used a variety of methods to communicate, and she felt "it forces you, as the teleworking employee, to be better at communicating" since you can't just go to your coworker's office to chat. Johnson's team used Skype for Business for calls, video conferencing, screen sharing, and instant messaging as well as email for longer, more detailed conversations.

Johnson stayed at home to work on her company-provided monitor, laptop, and keyboard, rather than going to a library or coffee shop on her teleworking weeks because of the sensitive information with which she worked. Though, those secure folders can present challenges to her productivity. Johnson highlights how the need for a good internet feed is paramount. If the connectivity wasn't great, she would end up refreshing and restarting a lot, which was disruptive.

Still, Johnson finds that though remote work isn't for everyone, it worked really well for her. "I can sit there for eight to nine hours a day and totally focus, but some others get super distracted," she says.

She attributes this to her preferred work style and the fact that she likes to work in a quiet environment. Johnson says she tends to find people distracting and the decrease in both the time and costs of commuting helped her overall productivity. Although her remote work plan with USCIS was short-term and she now works with another company, Johnson says she "would definitely do it again." She created her ideal experience by working within her company's existing remote work policy and then asking for the accommodation that fit her specific needs.

* * *

Johnson's experience ties together three of the five core elements that are essential to remote workers. When I spoke with her, she stated that she built her remote workspace based on the fact that...

1. She needed good connectivity to communicate with coworkers.

2. She worked with sensitive information and needed to use company-provided technology.

3. She couldn't focus well in noisy environments.

Johnson's work couldn't have been done in a noisy coffee shop where she was dealing with other people's sensitive information, so she needed the privacy of a home office with a private internet connection. Additionally, while some individuals love the constant hum of activity to keep them focused, it really bothered other people. Her ability to focus in a quiet environment isn't a trait that everyone possesses—as she acknowledged—but she recognized that it worked well for her.

ACCESS TO AMENITIES

The type of amenities that remote workers have access to are just as important as a break room stocked with snacks. Traditional offices invest in their workers in this way, and remote workers should build their remote workspaces with the same mentality. What allows you to boost your productivity? The thought that access to amenities matters in a remote worker space is only supported by the emergence of remote work programs like Remote Year.

Remote Year is built on the mentality that remote workers will be most productive when they have all of their basic needs (housing, travel, support, etc.) taken care of and met without worry. Even if you're not traveling the world, proximity to the bathroom, food, water, a gym, or another venue to stretch your legs can be a great way to stay happy while you're working. After all, this flexibility in many ways affords you the ability to create your own schedule. The amenities are a benefit of that, and you should take advantage of them.

* * *

Building your remote workspace relies on knowing what makes you tick. What will get you up and going in the morning? Why wasn't your traditional office space working for you? If you can build your picture perfect workspace (and you can!), what does it look like? Keep in mind the five core elements and get creative—for people like Greg Caplan, who started off in this exact same place, getting creative became his next great business venture.

CHAPTER 5

LEARN HOW TO BE MANAGED REMOTELY

—

If the office doesn't serve you as a worker, and you can be productive at home or anywhere else in the world, by all means look at leaving the office. But, don't forget about the office entirely and certainly don't forget about your team and manager, who connect you to some of the most important components of your role. After all, your job as a remote worker, whether you own a business or you're employed, is to make yourself visible and connected.

Visibility is a top issue in the remote work sector, and operating incorrectly once you're remote can put you on the chopping block (even at no fault of your own). Based on a study by Indeed, **nearly 40 percent of workers** felt that working remotely—despite having immense work-life balance benefits—hindered their ability to stay visible and even access leadership.[25] Possibly as a result of this obstacle, roughly one in four people who have the option to work remotely will still go into the office.

This might not sound promising for a budding remote work lifestyle, but combating these challenges isn't impossible. In fact, it comes down to using some HR-approved strategies to help improve visibility and availability.

Ringo Nishioka is the current VP of human resources and operations at Moxiworks and has worked in a variety of HR positions in Fortune 300 companies over the last fifteen years since graduating from Western Washington University with a degree in human resource management. He maintains his own blog, HRNasty, with over fifty thousand weekly subscribers and is cautious of the remote work scene.

"Remote employees can be successful, they just need to be very conscious of their career," he said.

Nishioka understands why individuals want to work from home. The convenience it offers is unparalleled. The benefits

---

25 "REPORT: Remote Work Can Bring Benefits, but Attitudes Are Divided." Indeed. http://blog.indeed.com/2018/11/14/remote-work-survey/ (June 17, 2019).

are valid. Yet, he finds that there is a disconnect in values in the workplace between those who want to work remotely and their supervisors. This ultimately creates an issue for how remote workers—or those wishing to go remote—are interacting with those who progress their career.

Ultimately, being successful as a remote worker comes down to understanding how to be managed remotely.

"Unfortunately, the decision makers in these companies are fifty to fifty-five years old, and it can be very difficult to convince a fifty-five-year-old exec," Nishioka says, "They'll tell you, 'I worked 80 hours a week, I didn't have a laptop, etc.' It's going to be a long time before a person coming right out of school can change that. The perspectives of the exec are the ones that matter because they are the one[s] who [are] controlling the situation."

Additionally, unless the remote worker has an incredibly scarce skill set, Nishioka noted that they are often the first to go when personnel cuts are made because they aren't visible and often aren't the people driving the culture in the office. The reasons that companies are resistant to a remote mentality is because of culture and energy. "They want a hustling, bustling, crowded, cramped office space because there is more energy in the office," he said.

Nishioka undoubtedly has a point. However, this isn't a story that you haven't heard previously. In fact, Anya Sanger and Erin Landis both gave glimpses into their stories on how generational divides impacted their remote work journey, and how you can continue to have effective relationships with coworkers and employees even from a distance. So, while those issues are present, that's nothing new. It's how you handle the situation once you're in it that really sets you apart.

Whether or not he finds remote work a personally compelling option as an HR professional or as a way to advance a career, Nishioka has been close to remote work through his wife. Nishioka said his own wife was provided the opportunity to work remotely because she had a scarce skill set in the tech industry. When this occurred, Nishioka provided advice to her from an HR perspective.

For one, Nishioka advised her to "manage her manager." This meant that she should brief her supervisor on exactly what she was going to accomplish on a weekly basis. Give him/her an update on Monday, and then at the end of the week, provide an update on the progress of her goals. Nishioka said that by doing this, you help mitigate the fear that many managers and colleagues have about remote workers. "What frustrates managers and colleagues is when they don't feel as though they know what a remote worker is doing. Our job is to make our manager's life easier. The last thing the manager wants to do is manage personal relationships," he said.

By providing a clear update about what you're doing—no matter where you are—you help demonstrate that you're on task and still working toward your goals as well as the company's goals.

The second piece of advice Nishioka provided his wife was to be in the office consistently and to make the days consistent as well. By doing this, you make your name and face known around the office despite not being there 80 percent of the time. Set up some time to go into the office during the workday to get to know your coworkers, and make it consistent so people know when to expect you if they need to collaborate on a project.

A bonus tip: Nishioka recommends also bringing a treat to the office at least once a month to help build these connections. Everyone loves the coworker in the office who brings in donuts or bagels, *but don't just leave them in the break room*.

Keep whatever you bring at your desk and send out an email to everyone that you brought in some treats and would love for people to stop by. This way, people have to engage, and you get some face time. Utilizing your time in the office like this is a sure-fire way to get to know coworkers better than you otherwise would have at home or just by sitting quietly in your cubicle when you're there sporadically.

So, how do you prevent yourself from being the first to go if you're a remote worker? You contribute to the culture and energy, AND you become a visibly effective worker. Despite not loving the idea of remote work, Nishioka offered solutions to all three of these "problems."

"One of the things we're doing to attract workers is offering remote work," he noted.

It's an attractive option, and while it's not for everyone, it could be for you. Find out what works for you and your company and work through the obstacles as they arrive. Being able to be managed remotely is integrally important to making a remote set-up function and flow.

It's part of what makes your work environment work for you. While the fifty-five-year-old exec might be running the office right now, we're only years away from promotions that put millennials in charge—individuals who grew up with laptops, instant messaging, and the freedom to create schedules on GCal that work for them. In some ways, it matters not where the workplace is now, but where it is going. The top talent controls the status quo, and the top talent is demanding remote work.

* * *

If and when you go remote, continue to impact your office. These spaces still exist, and they exist for good reason.

- Get to know your coworkers. Make yourself visible and available.

- Be in the office consistently so others can collaborate with and include you.

- Bring an occasional treat to facilitate engagement. It'll help you get to know others and make your presence memorable.

When you help create office culture and positive energy, you make yourself an attractive part of staff. Don't overlook the little actions you can take, even from afar.

PART 3

MANAGING REMOTELY

CHAPTER 6

FACILITATE BLENDED WORK

———

Blended workplaces are becoming more and more common. Workplaces are changing, and roughly 43 percent of offices have remote workers, which means that managers need to know how to balance and facilitate a blended workplace.[26] If there's one takeaway from this book, it's that remote work isn't for everyone. Remote workers will tell you this, I will tell you this, and you might find it out if you try it for yourself. Remote work can be challenging, and just like in any workplace setting, there are obstacles to combat.

———

26 Chokshi, Niraj. "Out of the Office: More People Are Working Remotely, Survey Finds." The New York Times. https://www.nytimes.com/2017/02/15/us/remote-workers-work-from-home.html (June 17, 2019).

In January 2019, the *New York Times* published an article called "The Death of the Sick Day."[27] Its contents are enough to make anyone think that remote work will leave you with *less* work-life balance than you had in the office. It discusses the challenges of having a sick day at all when one can simply work from home. With today's technology, there's no reason for someone not to be available when we have tools like email and Slack. Luckily, remote work experts are combating these issues within their very own teams, and as an employer, you can too.

This chapter will look specifically at the ways that remote work can challenge teams and the ways that employers can support and manage teams even when they include workers who operate differently. Having co-located (non-remote) and remote workers might mean that your office has to navigate some obstacles and challenges, but it doesn't mean that it can't function well, and perhaps even better than it did before, since every worker is getting what they need from their own work environment.

Remote work success is directly linked with how the work environment is set up (as we learned in Build Your Remote Workspace). Thus, in this chapter, we'll look at the advice of

---

27 Kurutz, Steven. "The Death of a Sick Day. The New York Times. https://www.nytimes.com/2019/01/10/style/the-death-of-the-sick-day.html (June 17, 2019).

three women who have managed and worked directly with remote workers. They discuss what works, what doesn't work, and how you can combat any challenges you encounter as a manager attempting to implement this in the workplace.

* * *

RESPECT THE TIME ZONE: MASTERING ASYNCHRONOUS COMMUNICATION

As an "agile coach" with the enterprise software company Sonatype, Susan Jasmin became a full-time remote employee three years ago, and she knows it's the way of the future. "This is how it's going to be in the future, with people moving to cities and how awful traffic is," she said.

Her process toward remote work began with baby steps. She first started working with offshore teams during her stint with National Geographic. For the first time, Jasmin experienced having colleagues in countries like India and Argentina, and even traveled to meet them. She said having the opportunity to meet those individuals in person gave her a new appreciation for those coworkers who were working remotely.

Shortly thereafter, Jasmin got the opportunity to experience remote work for herself. When a former boss called her up and offered her a job at Maryland-based Sonatype, Susan hesitated.

She was comfortable in Alexandria, Va., and couldn't imagine adding a lengthy commute through Washington, D.C., to her list of daily tasks. When her boss told her it would be a remote position, Jasmin's doubt disappeared immediately.

In her role at Sonatype, Jasmin now serves a variety of remote teams spanning several different time zones and has experienced just about every challenge that a remote worker might face, the largest being the adjustment to asynchronous communication. Anyone who has worked with colleagues in multiple time zones can relate to this battle. Jasmin says that "some people on my team are up and working for several hours before I start my day."

So, a big piece of this puzzle is figuring out how to work if you're in London and the information you need is from someone in Portland, where it's the middle of the night. Yet, being respectful of people's time zones is one of the factors that Jasmin said made Sonatype's remote culture work so well for the company.

Individuals don't have to worry about taking meetings over dinner or feeling as though they can't pick up their kids from the bus stop. In fact, Jasmin said the core component utilized in these cases was trust. If you're going to be unavailable, "just tell us when you're leaving" so everyone involved can feel comfortable with their schedule.

Now, in a workplace culture, this likely sounds unusual, even for co-located workers. It would seem inevitable that any given individual would have meetings that are slightly inconvenient or events that don't correspond with their outside obligations or their family's events. It's even more unusual in the remote workplace, where workers tend to feel as though they need to be online all the time in order to indicate that they're using their time productively and are available to their team, even though that's not always the case in an office setting.

Jasmin says, not only does she not feel as though she needs to be available at all hours when working remotely, but she also works hard to combat this with her teams in general. A couple of years ago, an individual who was leaving the company disclosed to her in their exit interview that this was one of his grievances with the company and position. Not being able to turn work off while at home really weighed on him. Since then, Jasmin has been really conscientious about making it easy for her team to indicate when they can participate, when they can't, and how to stay up to date if they aren't in all the meetings that happen outside their timezone.

For these purposes, Sonatype relies heavily on video conferencing and schedules all their meetings in Eastern Standard Time to accommodate the teams working from the West Coast as well as the United Kingdom. Their video conferences not only allow them to interface with team members who are thousands of miles away, but also permit them to disperse the recorded video once the session has finished. Jasmin said the ability to record team meetings or work demonstrations allowed for the asynchronous communication that enabled all these pieces to fit together.

Now, if this sounds too good to be true, you might be asking for the catch—there really isn't one. Jasmin says there are only two things you need to make this work: a good headset and solid Wi-Fi. That's it.

What about location? Are Sonatype employees limited as to where they can work? Not really. They like people who have worked remotely previously since they generally have a greater understanding of how to handle these factors and ask if you have a designated workspace, but they also understand the benefits that come with flexibility.

One UK team member spent six weeks in South Korea during the 2018 Winter Olympics last year, both working and traveling. His access to great Wi-Fi and communication made that trip possible. Another Canadian team member was in Spain for a month. He let his team know well in advance, and they were able to adjust meeting times to accommodate his new remote locale.

Of course, not everyone at Sonatype is traveling internationally, and more often than not this is just a great option for families, individuals unable or unwilling to commute, or people seeking a more flexible arrangement. However, it's still working. While Jasmin acknowledges it isn't for everyone, it really only takes a good headset and solid Wi-Fi to make it work if you want to.

Now, what's key to learning from Jasmin's situation as an employer is her mastery of asynchronous communication and her understanding that workers must have the ability to turn work off. Respect for remote workers' time is of the utmost importance. The fact of the matter is there should be an "out of office" even when your office is at home. Your remote workers will be far more willing to be in the office and have flexible hours beyond typical working hours if they do not feel that they are always on the clock. Case in point? Sick days should still exist.

Understanding that it isn't possible for someone to be up in the middle of the night on a conference call or miss dinner with their kids, simply because it works for the rest of the team, is important as a manager. What this means is that it is also incredibly important to establish the proper channels for workers to catch up on what they've missed. Successful remote teams create channels of transparency, which will be discussed in the next chapter.

SEEING REMOTE WHERE REMOTE CAN BE

Claire Kennedy is the senior director of people operations at Axios, and they've been building a remote culture from their 2016 onset. She said, "It's a thing that we do, for every role we ask, 'Can this person be remote?'"

Axios is an American news website and a company of 140 employees. Of those 140, fifteen are fully remote and working out of home offices across the United States.

Axios is still young. It was founded in 2016 by former Politico co-founder Jim VandeHei, Politico's former chief White House correspondent Mike Allen, and former Politico Chief Revenue Officer Roy Schwartz. Kennedy was working at Politico as a talent acquisition manager when the entirety of the senior leadership left in January 2016. She didn't hear what they were working on until August 2016, when they offered her a spot at Axios to help build a strong employer brand.

With that strong employer brand has come the remote work mentality for multiple reasons, the most important being the location of talent and diversity and inclusion.

While Washington, D.C., New York City, and San Francisco house Axios' three office locations, Kennedy recognizes that the talent Axios seeks is outside of these coastal cities as well. "We work in San Francisco, D.C., and New York and there's talent all over. We want to be able to hire talent where they are," she says.

Another factor that Kennedy says Axios incorporates is that of diversity and inclusion. She says that regional diversity is part of ensuring your staff is made up of a variety of different people. Recognizing that different types of thought proliferate in certain areas of the country and allowing workers from different areas to impact the company creates an overall more productive environment.

For these reasons, Axios has been positive about remote work from the get-go, but they're not so positive that they haven't revised their own model of remote work since their founding. "We have found massive pros, but we are starting to question the cons," Kennedy says.

Some positions aren't a good fit for the remote workplace, but the nature of others do lend themselves to being done in the field rather than in the office. For example, Kennedy says the fifteen who are currently remote full-time are engineers, designers, or reporters. The engineering team is the most dispersed of the three categories and Axios utilizes a couple of tactics to keep everyone connected.

One in particular that Kennedy stresses is a "new hire orientation" model. This is one that's been revised since they initiated a remote work culture. She says it used to be quite some time—even months—before new hires came to the headquarter locations to meet their colleagues after they began their role. Kennedy says this is, frankly, too much time to waste before people feel as though they're truly part of an organization.

The "new hire orientation model" is one where new hires come to what Kennedy calls the "mothership" for two full days within their first month of employment to meet individuals, hear the values and mission of the organization, and complete any remaining onboarding tasks. The new hire orientation is key to ensuring remote workers are off to a good start.

Axios also ships each remote worker a computer when they begin work to help keep them on track, and each employee receives the same IT support, regardless of whether they are remote or co-located. From a company standpoint, remote workers are treated like any other traditional worker. Yet, culturally, Kennedy acknowledged there are still challenges.

To keep them feeling connected, she said that remote workers were spotlighted in their internal newsletter each week to get their name and face out and about in the company sphere. They also use Donut, a Slack integration, which allows random employees to be paired every two weeks so they can meet up for coffee or another activity to get to know each other. Teams work over Slack, and every conference room is geared up with Zoom so all meetings have this capability. Management also ensures that business conversations are conducted 100 percent over one platform so no communication is lost for remote workers who can't have an in-person chats with their team to make a decision.

Still, Kennedy said, "When a team is not fully dispersed, it naturally allows for bonds to form and relationships to grow for some more than others."

Even if the nature of their work can be performed in the field, a partially versus fully distributed team can make a difference in how remote workers feel in relation to their company in teams.

Regardless, Kennedy said Axios will continue to hire more remote workers simply because of talent. She says the trend is growing, and it's important to not only support diversity and inclusion efforts regionally but also provide greater opportunity for women in the workplace with flexible schedules and the opportunity for expansion on both maternity and paternity leave.

Here, Kennedy highlights some of the crucial onboarding processes that can set remote workers on the right path. If your company is committed to making remote work an option for your employees, particularly because it's becoming more and more common as a talent acquisition strategy, then you'll want to ensure that you get them off to the right start. Your employees should absolutely feel connected to the office, whether or not they work in it everyday. It's essential for them to know their teams and to understand how the office setting works. Understanding the setup in the office will help them navigate any challenges they have remotely and know who their "point people" are.

Kennedy also highlighted an issue that can often arise in our technology-centered world. Think about your everyday life, particularly if you're under the age of 30. You likely use text message, phone calls, Snapchat, Facebook, Instagram, email, and numerous other platforms to communicate every single day. You use these platforms simultaneously, and it's likely you talk to the same people on more than one of these platforms. It's also likely you've gotten confused before about where you had a conversation and what was said. It happens. Having conversations on multiple platforms is difficult, and it's worse in the workplace when there are a number of players. Add in remote work, and you can easily get lost in a conversation. You could wake up to 50 messages on Slack and 35 emails and not know the best way to catch up.

Establishing clear lines of communication on how employees can gain access to information that they've missed if they weren't on a call or got lost in a string of messages is crucial to ensuring success for your team. As Kennedy mentioned, this problem can be resolved by establishing one platform as the method of communication, or perhaps even designating a point person as the individual to reach out to for communication questions or issues.

Finally, there's the issue of inclusion, and this is perhaps the most common issue that remote workers name time and time again. Being conscious of how your team operates, particularly if you're working with a team that is partially remote and partially co-located will be significant. You'll want to ensure that everyone feels connected since the typical "water cooler" feeling of an office is lost. Kennedy mentioned that Axios utilizes the Donut integration on Slack, and many remote workers highlighted this as a way that they have met people within their company. She also noted that the "new hire orientation" model can also help ease the disconnect between remote workers and their co-located counterparts. Invest in the onboarding process and don't forget to engage your remote workers after that as well.

IT'S ONLY GETTING EASIER

Emily Dresner is the chief technology officer at Upside Business Travel, a Washington, D.C., travel start-up that's built for business travelers to help them find the best deals and rewards. After a series of jobs in IT and network security as well as at video game companies and credit card agencies, she moved to Upside on February 17, 2016, while they were still in the development phase. In fact, they were still at the Dupont WeWork co-working space.

Upside does have an extensive remote work policy, but Dresner's contact with remote workers is rather light due to her position. However, her experience in managing remote teams came from her role with Fugue, a Maryland-based start-up that automates cloud operations, a job that she held directly prior to joining Upside.

"I had this problem at Fugue because we had remote workers all over the world," she said, "How do you keep these people in the loop, informed, and remind the team that they exist? How do you ensure they have a voice? And that they know what decisions have been made?"

This is a problem that a lot of companies who are entirely or partially remote face, and it can be aided by the technology that now permeates the workspace.

"It's easier today than it was four years ago," Dresner said.

She noted two pieces of technology that are paramount for remote workspaces. One is having access to calls. Two is a video conferencing platform. Teleconferencing is crucial because it provides an avenue for everyone to be conscientious of the people who are or are not in every single meeting that is held. "Slack also helps but isn't a perfect tool," she said.

While Slack is often glorified in the remote workspace, Dresner emphasized more direct communication. "Having a touch point every single day is important," Dresner said, "We try to stay away from email. It's very slow and it's a big effort to answer an email. It's also very easy to ignore, delete, or walk away from."

Dresner said that reading fifty lines of Slack is much more doable in the remote workspace, or really any workspace, than a fifty-chain email. In fact, she said, "Often what happens is people say 'Can someone DM me a summary?' if they missed the conversation as it was happening."

Dresner's analysis of the greatest issues in remote work extend far beyond the technology. She's hitting on the tough cultural aspects that almost every remote worker has felt. The inability to be in the office and be present at every meeting often results in a remote worker being or feeling a step behind the rest of their coworkers. Her suggestions stem directly from the effort to bring these individuals into the fold and ensure the company collectively is (and coworkers individually are) thinking conscientiously about those who aren't immediately present but are just as important to the smooth operation of the business.

On the flipside, there's another cultural problem that accompanies remote work once the companies figure out the connectivity issues. Dresner said, "The biggest issue is for remote workers to be painfully and excruciatingly conscious of being on call."

So, it becomes a balance. Ensuring that you bring individuals from the outside into the fold, but don't put them on the spot all the time when it's outside working hours or when co-located employees otherwise wouldn't be "on call" either.

Dresner is incredibly real about the obstacles in remote work. She didn't shy away from the challenges that she experienced when managing remote teams. Yet, she did highlight some of these challenges and how she dealt with them. We're already familiar with the issue of remote workers missing out on information and feeling as though they must be "on call." The best remedies to these situations are open communication with your workers. Ensuring that they know that they can reach out if they missed something in the workplace and knowing who to reach out to is crucial. Likewise, having the same expectations for remote workers that you would for co-located workers is something that cannot be forgotten. Just because remote workers have all the resources that they need to continue to work at home after hours doesn't mean there should be any more of an expectation than there is for co-located workers. If your company policy is that leaving the office means you leave the work with you, allow your remote workers to clock out as well. It'll make them better and more productive workers when they are "in the office."

* * *

Despite the challenges discussed in this chapter, there are ways to combat obstacles that arise, particularly in how you set up your team initially. Chapter 7: Learn How to Manage Remote Workers will discuss the key elements of successful remote teams and how you can implement that setting. At its core, it's all about understanding and respecting the remote worker's workspace and implementing tools and resources that allow them to get what they need from the workplace and you as a manager.

CHAPTER 7

LEARN HOW TO MANAGE REMOTE WORKERS

────

The initial setup of the remote team (or teams) in your workplace can make or break how successful a company becomes. Managing remotely is about supporting your employees where they are currently at, and most companies who have done it successfully have discovered and implemented a number of shared elements.

This chapter will explore those specific elements and the suggested tactics and strategies of successful remote workplaces. You'll hear from HR professionals who have made it their mission to create inclusive work environments for both co-located employees and remote workers. With loneliness, lack of collaboration, and communication issues being problematic for **one in five remote workers,** management can now do more to help resolve these problems—even from a distance.[28] What's more is that workers now have an expectation that this type of management should be in their supervisor's role. Given the influence remote workers now have on office settings and within teams, even non-remote employees now believe that managers should have knowledge of how to manage blended teams.

YOUR ROLE DOESN'T MATTER, YOUR RESOURCES DO

As the director of talent at Upside Business Travel, Hilliary Turnipseed has been in talent acquisition for a little over ten years now. She's worked at companies like Politico and Discovery Communications, and a lot of her focus has been on onboarding, acquiring talent, and ensuring that employee skill sets match the needs of the company. She knows what it means to set employees up for success and what common tools and resources they need to ensure positive outcomes in the workplace. Turnipseed also knows that remote work is not only the way of the future, but that it also takes on many forms.

---

28 Morris, Zoe. "How to Keep Your Remote Workers From Feeling Isolated." TLNT: Talent Management & HR. https://www.tlnt.com/how-to-keep-your-remote-workers-from-feeling-isolated/ (June 17, 2019).

"Remote work is, I think, where the [technology] industry is headed," she said, which makes sense given Upside Business Travel's hearty remote work policy.

Turnipseed explained the policy: "Our philosophy is that, as long as your performance is not an issue, and you are providing everything that your immediate team needs, that we don't care where you're doing it from."

This policy isn't limited to roles in the technology industry. Turnipseed went as far as to say, "You could literally do most roles, anywhere. I could do my role anywhere."

Your role doesn't matter in the remote workspace, but what does matter is your resources and your links to the office, as well as your attitude toward the culture you're creating as a remote worker. When Turnipseed thinks of remote work, she thinks of both partially remote situations as well as fully remote situations. Upside handles employees with both arrangements. While roughly 99 percent of Upside's personnel is in D.C., none of the workers are required to be in the office all day, every day. That said, only about two individuals in the entire company are entirely remote, 100 percent of the time.

"The 100 percent remote work situation is where I try to focus on making sure that [remote workers] have resources and links to the office," she said, "Everything we do from a company-wide standpoint on a day-to-day is to make it as accessible as possible to people who aren't here."

Well, technology is a huge component. "Everything that we do here really happens in Slack and document sharing. It doesn't really matter if you're in the office or not," she said.

Slack channels are used for anything from business meetings to social gatherings. Upside uses Donut, a free Slack integration, to pair up three people at the company every four weeks. Turnipseed said, "It's a way that people who might not necessarily work together on a day-to-day to get to know each other more," and about 80 percent of their employees use it regularly.

Additionally, for meetings, Turnipseed said that they just dial people in on Zoom if they're not physically present. But what if people just don't answer? Has that ever been an issue?

"It depends on the company. Being at a start-up or small company, it's very hard to disappear," she said.

Upside doesn't allow individuals to just fall off the grid. Their company culture isn't built for no-shows. Once you're onboard, your position from an employee standpoint has clear expectations, another recommendation of Turnipseed.

"It's really important that, as a remote employee, you're setting yourself up for success and that you're also being a strong performer for your company," she said.

Being clear on expectations, being accessible, being communicative, being transparent, being open, and demonstrating high performance is imperative.

These traits are seen in those two individuals who work 100 percent remotely for Upside. Turnipseed says they are consultants who are "really, really good at their jobs, really accessible, and really communicative."

These individuals have open calendars, are clear about when they'll be accessible and when they won't be, and provide deliverables that keep the company on track.

For individuals desiring to move toward this type of arrangement, whether partially or fully, Turnipseed said it's all about how you deliver, and this may delay your remote start initially. She suggests getting a strong footing in the office through the onboarding process for at least a month or so. After that, you can work toward the flexible work arrangements that best suit your schedule and personal life.

Upside understood the benefit of flex schedules and worked to integrate these individuals into the office space every day with the help of their remote employees.

"I think it's really that the expectations are clear from the employer and employee. The level of transparency and communication. People have different needs, but if you're delivering in the way your teams need you to deliver then it works."

The key elements that Turnipseed implements for her employees starts from a place that most employers don't even consider. She skips the mentality that "this role must do this or that" in order to be successful. As long as an individual is delivering in their role, it's about the resources and expectations that a manager provides from the onset that allows success for both sides. The proper tools and dedicated workspace discussed in Chapter 4 and 5 are key to ensuring that workers know how to communicate effectively and efficiently. For those in the remote work sphere, it's not about the work itself but about how the work gets done.

FIND THE RIGHT LEADERSHIP AND THE RIGHT PLATFORMS

Karina Miller is the managing director of Swift HR Solutions in Portland, Ore., and CEO Shannon Swift has dubbed her the "virtual client HR queen." She fell into remote work fairly early on in her career after joining Swift HR Solutions.

The need for working remotely in Miller's life really came from a personal place.

"I was 25 when I had my first kid, and I had a long commute in order to afford where I lived," she said.

Miller noted that raising kids with a long commute and a professional career is incredibly challenging. While her commute allowed her to make ends meet, it wasn't at all practical for parenting purposes. "I was over an hour from my child's daycare," she remembered.

Anyone who has been a parent or worked with kids knows this: Kids can get sick or hurt, and daycares can close unexpectedly. Stuff happens, and getting a call from your kid's daycare in the middle of the workday when it's an hour away is a nightmare. Miller noted that this is an issue for the majority of mothers in the workplace, and a reason why women who hit the glass ceiling end up starting their own business. It becomes difficult to create a balance that works for them, their personal life, and their career.

Then, Miller joined Swift HR Consulting, and her work life changed dramatically. The model of Swift HR Consulting is like most other consulting firms. They work onsite with their clients. Yet, Miller ended up with a virtual client that had no office at all. As that company worked remotely, so did Miller.

Miller began to learn how to function in a remote work setting from her client, while also consulting them on how to support their business goals. She said this particular client, whom she cannot name without permission, "has it set up perfectly." For our purposes, we'll call the company "Russet."

"I did everything to support what they'd already created and then helped come up with new ideas as well," she said.

The organization that Russet had already created was built on a single value: trust. Miller said this is paramount because CEOs fundamentally distrust employees and believe that people will take advantage of both them and the system. To help mitigate this fear, they look for a particular type of employee. Employees who are great fits for remote roles are often those who already have experience working remotely and are mature enough to work independently.

The company, as a whole, also fosters the ability to make remote work functional as well. Miller says, "Working remotely is vastly better if the whole company is virtual."

But, why is this? Is it possible to make it work if you're the only one at your company who is working remotely? Yes, it is, but there are two key factors that any remote worker will need to keep in mind.

1. It will probably be an uphill battle

2. Remote work is better with the right leadership

For the first factor, Miller said it'll be an "uphill battle for anyone at the company to include you" if you're the only one working remotely. In fact, it's quite easy for individuals to feel left out when they're the only one not at the office. Coworkers often forget to invite remote workers to events due to sheer complacency, and it's easy to feel left out because of this. Remote workers don't have the opportunity to engage in any water cooler issues. Yet, if any of this is voiced, Miller said remote workers often face backlash: "You're going to come across as a complainer and a whiner."

Inevitably, there can be resentment in the office because you get to work from home. For many, it's a desirable convenience. Having the leverage to advocate for yourself while at home isn't going to be the easiest experience, however. Miller also noted that remote workers don't get a lot of sympathy from management if the entire company isn't working remotely. She said she's encountered executives in the past who have thought, "Well, I'm not going to give them as big of a raise because they work from home and don't have to pay for commuting, dry cleaning, etc."

While this may sound exceedingly frustrating, it leads right into Miller's second factor: management. Working under the right leadership in any position is important, but it is absolutely essential when it comes to working remotely.

"You can be doing a fantastic job, and they will be looking for all the reasons to back up what they already think," Miller said.

This is especially true if you're the only one, or one of the few, in your office space who is doing it. If leadership is cautionary to begin with, it might not be the right work environment for you. What you bring to the table is important—for example, those with more specific skill sets typically have more leverage because they're harder to replace—but it's not the be-all and end-all if your environment doesn't support your work habits.

Miller said that once you're in this position, you'll need to work hard to build relationships and create facetime, which probably sounds difficult with the lack of office time. However, she encouraged coworkers who live and work nearby to build "unconventional relationships" through happy hours, lunches, or coworking opportunities.

Now, how has this played out in Miller's own work and career? Not only is she consulting on remote work with virtual clients, but she herself is working remotely. After she was given Russet as a client, she was slowly given more and more virtual clients because she knew how to handle them. Miller said it worked great because when she moved, she only lost one client because of the arrangement.

"Now I have 100 percent remote clients. Only one has an office space," she says.

Miller didn't have to work onsite with clients who don't have office spaces, so she has had the opportunity to discover firsthand the best remote worker hiring practices, best remote platforms, and best tactics for creating a cohesive work environment.

Yet, remember that remote work isn't functional for everyone. When Miller looks for people to hire, she frequently starts by testing them out as contractors, often on a trial basis. In the interviews themselves, she also utilizes case interviews to help screen individuals and see if they are a good fit when dealing with scenarios common to remote workers.

She's found that certain platforms are predominant in the remote workplace as well. Slack, integrated with Google Hangouts, and Zoom, utilized for video calls, are vital for everyday use. Miller encourages companies to have a "team speaking" function for phone calls with a "push to talk" feature. Having to opt into talking instead of needing to mute everyone reduces the amount of noise from kids, dogs, construction, or other miscellaneous background noise.

To raise morale, which can be difficult when a team is entirely remote, Miller has relied on her connection to Zoom quite a bit to foster community. When team members are first onboarded, she has them fill out a survey about their food, restaurant, and gift preferences. Then, as the holidays come around, Miller utilizes this information to get creative.

"For example, in the past, I've sent everyone a little care package with hot cocoa and a dice game. I tell everyone to wait to open it until we're on Zoom, then they can make the hot cocoa and drink it while everyone plays a few games with the dice on Zoom," she said.

Miller is demonstrating that all the "fun" parts of an office don't have to stop just because you're virtual. The functionality of Zoom allows there to be different channels and breakout rooms. She'll have people submit photos around the holidays for photo contests, they'll do trivia contests over breakout rooms, or she'll send gift cards for anniversaries.

While she says it can be a little harder to work on the road, Miller says she absolutely loves working remotely. She saves so much time and is able to bring all these innovative ideas to a virtual space. Her situation necessitated a change many years ago, and now she's making it possible for others to engage in a different type of workspace as well.

Miller's brought her own flair to remote work and attempts to make the remote workspace a little bit smaller with some of those "in-office perks" for those who are out of the office. Isolation and loneliness is one of the reasons why it's so important to find those managers who can make your team feel like a team. By integrating games, gift cards, and photo contests into your remote office in a natural way, you're helping your remote workers feel a little less like they're doing it all on their own.

HOW TO BUILD A REMOTE SETTING THAT WORKS

The lessons that Turnipseed and Miller learned through trial and error are those that can be implemented in remote work settings across the world to help create unique workspaces that foster collaboration between the employer and their employees. Follow the guidelines below to apply some of the best elements into the remote setting.

1) TRANSPARENCY

Creating a culture of transparency from the start is the first way that you can build a remote setting that works for you and that works for your remote employees. Start with the new hire orientation model that Claire Kennedy spoke about that allows everyone to get onboard and on the same page. This will give your remote employee a chance to understand the expectations that you have and for them to also share their needs with you.

Next, set your employees up for success by ensuring that they have the right equipment for their position. You heard Susan Jasmin talk about how success comes down to being well-equipped. This includes laptops, headsets, Wi-Fi, productive workspaces, etc. (whatever that may look like for your employees). These are all important and having them from the onset of the role will make all the difference.

Finally, institute a model of regular visits to the office (if your company has one). Make it flexible for the worker, but if this is something you, as manager, would like to see then make sure the remote worker knows that. The won't be able to accommodate, deliver or voice concerns with visits to the office if you don't clarify whether or not it is something you're seeking.

2) IMPROVEMENT

Remote work cultures are ones that can constantly seek improvement. Ensure success by instituting a culture in which your employees and management feels as though they can constantly strive for improvement. Your approach can be experimental. Let everyone know that you're still learning and that you want to ensure that changes can be made if someone doesn't feel that a practice is working.

For instance, if you're in an office setting that allows a flexible remote work arrangement (employees can utilize the office space but can also work remotely), let your employees know that they can head out of the office space if they don't feel that their time is being maximized. This will allow everyone the space to figure out what works best for them. Remember, you can do most jobs anywhere. As long as employees are getting their work done, it doesn't matter where they're doing it.

3) COMMUNICATION

Establishing clear communication channels is a primary responsibility of you, as the employer. In part, this will need to be done in the initial stages of onboarding. Delineating a hierarchy of needs and providing information to your employees on exactly who can serve as resources to them remotely will aid both you and your employees so that you can all coordinate efficiently. For instance, if you're working across a variety of time zones and a remote worker happens to miss a meeting, who is their established contact to get caught up? Who will send a followup email with any missed or need-to-know information? Consider implementing a co-pilot or a buddy system that allows the remote worker to have an individual that they can fall back on. Eliminate that common issue of, "We have all these channels, and I don't have any idea where to look." Get creative. Always record meetings, send out an email, write blogs, or follow up in another way to ensure that communication is clear even if you're not present.

Additionally, highlight again and again that asking questions in a public channel, such as Slack, is encouraged. Often remote employees may not want to seem behind or unaware, even if they are because they were accidentally left out of the loop. Opening up the ability to ask questions publicly (without shame) will enhance communication and coordination while improving your company's overall efficacy.

Finally, the tools that remote workers use (Slack, email, Google Drive, IM, internal company systems, etc.) are crucial to their success. Allow your team a choice in selecting the tools that they use. Having ineffective tools or tools that simply do not work for the team will create problems from the onset. Avoid this by allowing your employees to have an active hand and ownership over choosing them.

4) RESILIENCE

Remote workers require support within their management to maintain resilience when things get off track. Resilience in the workplace, particularly a remote workplace, means creating an adaptive environment where you can adjust to a hardship quickly and recalibrate to meet goals. Resilience has much to do with how much control a team has over their (virtual) workplace. It relies on ownership over communication. Can anyone begin a new communication channel at any given time or can only management initiate communication? Even if they are "capable," is there psychological safety in doing so? Is there a culture that encourages it?

Additionally, can anyone facilitate a meeting? Employees who gain confidence and support at work from their supervisors by volunteering to facilitate meetings. Yet, opportunities like this do not exist unless management works to integrate them. Promoting a holistic culture with a work-life balance that provides agency to remote workers will ultimately make them more resilient in situations that present obstacles.

5) COLLABORATION

Workplaces are intended to foster collaboration, and remote workplaces can provide the very same collaborative environment with the correct setup and proper tools in place. Collaboration permits teams to explore problems and solutions more quickly and efficiently. Collaboration acknowledges the work-life balance of the individual and implements solutions like asynchronous communication. Even if your employees' full eight-hour work days don't overlap entirely, they still have set time for solo and collaborative work. Time zone differences are only a barrier if you make them a barrier.

Overall, does your team feel supported? Remember your responsibility as management is to bring people in outside their role as an employee. Karina Miller goes as far as to use Zoom as a way to create a holiday party atmosphere. She sends out care packages with food and games that allow people to engage in team bonding. Don't forget what sometimes gets lost in a remote setting, and remember that you're caring for these individuals and their happiness as employees as well—even if you don't see them in the office every day.

* * *

Managing remotely may initially feel challenging for those who have only onboarded and supervised co-located employees. Yet, as remote work has increased by 140 percent in the last fifteen years, it's quickly becoming the work style of the future. In fact, 90 percent of remote workers plan to be remote for the rest of their lives.[29] These employees aren't going anywhere, and neither are their employers. Discovering ways to build a remote setting that works in your office opens your company up to greater success in the future by encouraging greater diversity and attracting more robust talent. Knowing how to facilitate these settings is no longer a bonus—it's a requisite.

29 Caramela, Sammi. "Communication, Technology, and Inclusion Will Shape the Future of Remote Work." Business News Daily. https://www.businessnewsdaily.com/8156-future-of-remote-work.html (June 17, 2019).

PART 4

WINNING REMOTELY

CHAPTER 8

HOW TO PITCH REMOTE WORK TO YOUR EMPLOYER

This chapter might very well be the reason that you picked up this book, and I won't hold out on you much longer. Pitching remote work to your employer won't ever be an exact science because every company is different, yet following the playbook in this chapter will give you tried and true guidelines from remote workers around the world. It'll also give you a head start in knowing exactly how to pitch your remote work journey to your boss.

Before you see the "playbook" itself, let's look at a couple more stories of workers who've pitched their situation without even knowing if their pitches would work. While they didn't have any other options at the time, the tactics they used were sound. They found out what works in real-work settings because they simply didn't have another choice. Knowing what they did can help you develop your own winning strategy to create a workplace that's right for you.

SAMARA WENTEN

Samara Wenten is coming up on her ten-year anniversary of working remotely. "I've worked from home since 2009. That bridges three homes, fives jobs, a high-risk pregnancy and birth, and now have a full-time family. It's the best. I can't imagine doing it another way," she said.

Yet, Wenten's path to remote work didn't begin as a linear process. She started out as a middle school teacher for high-risk students, and at the end of a really tough year, she decided to take a break. Wenten wanted to work in education, but she didn't want to leave her house. Amazingly, that's when her cousin proposed a solution that changed Wenten's career path. A Massachusetts-based start-up was looking for a point person to head up operations on the West Coast. The industry? Education technology, a field right in Wenten's wheelhouse.

Wenten took the position and was suddenly doing exactly what she wanted when she took a break from teaching: working in education but doing it from home. She followed the company through an acquisition and continued to work remotely, either from home or in cities around the US when she would travel to occasional conferences, retreats, and meetings.

Then, Wenten got recruited to a different start-up in San Francisco, but she didn't want to give up the remote work lifestyle she had already built.

She told the company point blank, **"I don't go into an office, I work from home."**

Their response? "You can work from anywhere as long as you can get your work done."

Wenten attributes this work schedule flexibility to a "Silicon Valley ethos" and notes just how many individuals take advantage of it at her current company, Salesforce.com; there aren't even assigned desks, just an open workspace for those who choose to come into the office. As a Senior Solution Engineer for Higher Ed, she doesn't think she'll return full-time at the office anytime soon.

"I just don't see myself doing it while my daughter is young," she said.

Right now, she goes into the office once or twice a week and enjoys doing so, it's just not convenient. Her commute is twenty-five to sixty minutes on the bus, depending on traffic, and the time it takes to get ready is time that's tough to come by as the mother of an elementary schooler. She might miss the company holiday party or the occasional catered lunch, but those trade-offs don't compare to the time and flexibility she gains from her ability to work remotely. Working remotely allows her to take her daughter to school and work comfortably from her home office.

Along with the Silicon Valley ethos, Wenten's willingness to take that initial risk, her persistence through numerous work and personal situations, and her ability to find what truly works for her in the workspace continues to make her remote career not only attainable, but fulfilling.

MELISSA JOHNSON

Earlier in Chapter 5, we heard from Melissa Johnson, the Georgetown alum who reached a compromise with USCIS to work remotely while she relocated to the greater Boston Area. She found that her workspace benefited from a home office environment, but the way that she came to that arrangement is something we all can learn from.

Since her situation didn't align with her company's telework policy, she needed to liaise with her supervisors. Johnson described USCIS's current remote work policy as: "You're not supposed to telework more than five days in a pay period that is fourteen days, and no more than three days in a week."

So, while there was a remote work policy in place that Johnson knew of, it wasn't flexible enough to help her with her relocation. Yet, through a series of exchanges with her supervisor and a couple levels of senior management, Johnson was able to have a special exception made for her, just by having the conversation.

She arranged a one-week-on, one-week-off remote work policy that eased the amount of commuting she'd have to do to continue to work at USCIS. To arrange it, she went to her supervisor, conveyed her situation, and told him she'd have to find another job because she was moving. Instead of doing that, however, she ended up going through senior management and then even another level to discuss her situation and how she could make it work. Finally, through this hierarchy, it got approved. Johnson says the hierarchical approval was necessary so that they "knew I wouldn't take advantage of it."

She created her ideal experience by working within her company's existing remote work policy and then asking for an accommodation that fit her specific needs. While it took some time to get it approved through the structure of her company, it wasn't impossible; it just needed some time to work its way through the hierarchy. Johnson's ability to ask for what she needed and talk to those who could make it happen ultimately resulted in a work situation that made her a more productive and content worker.

THE PLAYBOOK

SETTING THE STAGE

Paul Carney is the senior vice president of human resources at Carter Bank & Trust. He's had a long history of entrepreneurship. He started his first company in 1996 after writing a computer program, and then started another in 1999 after selling the first company. Carney made the jump to HR with Navy Federal Credit Union in 2012, which provided learning and development training in the field. While he was there, Carney learned a lot about HR, earned his certification, and also observed the fact that the HR division wasn't being managed like a business.

As a result of his experience, Carney authored a book—*Move Your Æ (ash): Know, Grow, and Show Your Career*

Value—on taking ownership, managing, and being in charge of your career.

In the experience that led to this book, particularly working with Natural Insights, where he was a vice president of technical services, Carney got to know the business of working remotely and the impact this phenomenon had on the inner workings of companies.

"It's a cultural transformation for most organizations to have remote workers," he said.

Thus, Carney advocates looking at HR as a business in order to get a spot at the table with senior leadership. This includes looking at human resources and employees themselves as a business. Carney is, of course, referring to the model that IBM implemented about five to ten years ago. The company shifted everyone out to a remote work setting in order to save money on rent.

But here's the catch: Just like working in an office isn't effective for everyone, neither is remote work. Thus, this didn't ultimately end up being an effective method to drive business or save money, and IBM just ended up pulling everyone back into the office.

He said, "If you're sending them out to be remote because you think it'll save you money, it generally isn't the right model. You have to look at how it increases motivation."

While this is valuable insight for any company, it's also just as valuable for a worker desiring to go remote. How do you design a successful pitch to your company about making your work remote? Carney said it's about creating a *business case* and presenting it to your employer.

"It's not so much about a case of cutting the costs," he said, "It has to orient itself to the remote worker being a return on an investment."

Your pitch to go remote should be a case about driving higher motivation. It should improve your work environment, improve your concentration, improve your motivation, and therefore, drive higher business outcomes. **Your pitch should look at how you're adding value to the company by creating a situation that works better for you.** This type of approach will likely garner a better reaction.

Ultimately, employees who aren't engaged and communication that isn't working well won't drive better business outcomes.

Carney says that it's all about ensuring that both sides know what will improve the business, "Making sure that employees understand the value they're adding to the organization and organizations understand the value employees add for them."

THE PITCH

When pitching remote work to your employer, remember the acronym "EPPE." It'll help you see your situation as it is, understand your prospects for success, consider how to move forward, and know what motivates the person sitting at the other side of the table. It'll demonstrate the proper way that you can set up a successful pitch and lay out the crucial elements that many of the case studies in this book just so happened to implement themselves.

As Carney pointed out, your company is a business and approaching personnel issues like HR as a business can help you get to where you want to be. In this case, you want your boss to help you, and the way to do that isn't by cutting costs (which might seem like the obvious pitch) but by helping them to see how this change *makes you a better worker.*

EVALUATION

The first E in EPPE stands for evaluation. Evaluating your situation at your company, you individual role, or both can make or break a successful pitch. This is what Laura Meier-Schmitz, Erin Landis, Samara Wenten, and Melissa

Johnson did. They knew that their workplaces weren't working for them, and they didn't hesitate to evaluate what would make them more productive. This part of the process is all about evaluating your needs as a worker.

What will serve you in your work environment? Do you have it in your current office? Could you get it in a home office? Could you get it on the road? In a coffee shop? In a mix of environments? Is there something holding you back from being productive? Your home life, a commute, distractions in the office? Evaluate your current situation and begin to document how you think a different environment could serve you.

PREPARATION

The documentation that you make in your "Evaluation" stage will be helpful here. Preparation is all about taking the right steps to ensure that your management takes you seriously. When you pitch your remote work journey to your employer, you want to ensure that you have the proper documentation.

Do you have previous experience working remotely? Do you spend a certain number of hours commuting that could otherwise contribute to company productivity? Do you have another need that isn't being met by the 9-to-5 lifestyle? Your pitch should not only benefit you as a worker, but also your company, so be sure to think about the process holistically.

Think through exactly what working remotely would look like. What type of support would you need from your current team? How would it change office life for the individuals you work with? How would you make yourself available and ensure that you're still delivering all your work as if you're in the office?

These are likely questions you'll be asked when you meet with your supervisor. Think about it during your preparation phase so as to avoid being unprepared on the spot.

PRESENTATION

This is probably the part that you're dreading, but if you've correctly evaluated the situation and properly prepared, then the presentation is just the next right step. Ask to meet with your supervisor in a one-on-one setting. If you already have a weekly one-on-one or some type of built-in check-in, then that can be a great time to do it. Remember, this request is about improving your productivity and making you a better worker. In the end, it should be a mutually beneficial arrangement.

When you present this idea to your boss, be sure to lay out your concerns about your current work situation. Discuss HOW it is impacting your work productivity and how you can think it might be improved with a separate arrangement.

If you have an existing policy at your work that you're looking to amend (like Johnson did), then you can work off of that.

Be ready to demonstrate that you've thought this through. Discuss how you'll continue to impact the office. Will you still come to the office part of the time? How will you make yourself available to your team? Alleviate any concerns up front and be open to what your supervisor has to say as well.

EXECUTION

Once you've presented your pitch to your supervisor, a number of things could happen. You could get an immediate "YES!" This happened to several of the case studies in this book. Their bosses were so desperate to keep them in their position that they said yes immediately...even if they probably weren't supposed to.

You could also get deferred, which doesn't necessarily mean 'no.' It just means that your supervisor may not have the immediate authority to allow you to work remotely. Don't panic! Continue to have the conversation. Get visibility with your boss's boss and address their concerns up front. The more people you have onboard with you in the beginning, the more likely you are to be successful in the long run. You want to make sure you communicate your needs and put your (and the company's) productivity first.

To see how EPPE looks in real life, we'll look at a case study of another woman who fell into remote work and did an incredible job of advocating for herself throughout the entire process, one who hasn't stopped yet.

EPPE IN REAL-LIFE

Natalie White has been in the remote work game for seven years now, and she attributes her success to the name she built for herself in the workplace before going remote. She worked hard to ensure that she was visible, reliable, and vocal about her accomplishments.

"Building that credibility is part of the reason they were willing to let me work full-time remotely," she said. And that tactic hasn't stopped since she moved to a home office.

She started out at an e-commerce payment company called CyberSource, now owned by Visa, in 2010. They're headquartered in Mountain View, Calif., with a satellite office in Boulder, Calif., but White was located in Fort Worth, Texas. She worked there for five years, leading business engagement, requirements gathering, and technical implementation of custom e-commerce payment solutions for customers. She traveled about 20 percent of the time for that job.

In 2015, White left CyberSource/Visa and actually returned to an office setting at a small to mid-sized pharmacy software company called PDX. Headquartered in Fort Worth, Texas, where she was still living at the time, White had the opportunity to take advantage of their optional three-day-a-week home work policy. Yet, the office was convenient, so she typically went into work except on Fridays.

Then, White's husband was offered a job in Southern California in 2017, so she decided to ask if she could work remotely full-time. She went into her then-direct manager and told him that her husband got a new job which was great but...

"And he said, 'Oh my gosh, please don't leave,'" she recalled. "He thought it was going to be a resignation and then I asked to work remotely full-time."

White continues that her manager responded, "Yes, of course, yes," on the spot...and then maybe asked for approval later, but it was never an issue. In fact, she already had some visibility with his managers, so once White got the approval, everything was in motion from there. PDX even bought her a laptop before she left so that she could complete her work from home without technological hiccups.

After beginning her 100 percent remote work venture, White found out that she wasn't the only one of PDX's 500-600 employees who was working from home full-time in the United States. There were about twelve fully-remote workers then.

In fact, another one of her PDX coworkers had created a fully remote arrangement when his wife had a baby. White remembered the "he wanted to do it temporarily to bond with the baby and help her, and then he never came back" from his remote work setup.

The success that White and her colleague had during their remote ventures helped to create a new PDX policy. White said, "Because of the success we've had proving to the company that we can be just as, if not more, productive working remotely, they recently updated their policy to allow anyone to work remotely full-time as long as they get their work done and it works for their team."

White noted the caveat that it doesn't work for everyone for social and travel-related reasons.

"In general, working remotely doesn't work for everyone. It can, like my first job, mean you're required to travel more. It can be extremely isolating, as it is for me now, where I have to get on a plane to see my coworkers in the office. To mitigate that I will sometimes go work at a coffee shop to break up the monotony of being at home all the time."

White said she tries to go to a library or a coffee shop at least once a week, and on the weeks she doesn't do it, she ends up feeling kind of stuck because her children, aged four and seven, keep her home at night. Fortunately, flexible childcare arrangements like a gym with childcare resources and a cafe to work make it possible for her to get out and about after her kids are home from school.

This ability really improves her work-life balance as well. While she's firm that she wouldn't be able to work remotely if she kept her kids at home with her, White recognized the benefit that the additional time can bring to accommodating some of those household duties.

"It can be a wonderful benefit to employees as well. With no commute, I can keep up with home duties a lot more effectively. I can be on a conference call from anywhere, and the flexibility it has given me and my family has been invaluable, especially after we had kids."

White was a reliable employee in the office and that enabled her to secure her remote position when she needed to leave the co-located office for her husband's relocation. Yet, being visible and vocal about their work and accomplishments is something that remote workers can have difficulty doing because, well, they aren't visible. You heard in Chapter 8 how ardently Ringo Nishioka argued for certain actions as a remote worker. While he remained cautious that visibility and generational divides could hinder remote workers, White has used it to fuel her.

During our chat, she referred to an organization she's part of called the Society of Women Engineers. It's one of the activities that help get her out a couple nights a month when she feels like she hasn't had enough human contact, but it's also provided her a space to dialogue how to track her progress in her company.

White said, "Women think, 'Well if I just keep my head down and do my part then I'll be recognized and compensated,' but it's just not true."

She urges employees—remote or not—to be vocal about their accomplishments and value to management because sometimes there aren't built-in opportunities to demonstrate it. At PDX, there aren't performance reviews or specific times to ask for additional compensation if you feel it's warranted.

If this sounds a little scary, there are a couple of ways you can come up with concrete evidence of how you're performing well and adding value to a company:

1. **Keep an accomplishment journal.** White said, "One of the ways I do this is that I keep a digital journal that I

write in at least twice a week. I write what I did and certain accomplishments during a release cycle." Keeping this journal will help you remember if you get stuck in the day-to-day. When you reflect on what you've done, you can say, "I think it's about time for a raise," based on the concrete accomplishments you've recorded in this journal.

2. **Volunteer for roles that get your name out there.** We already saw how this worked for White earlier when her manager's supervisor approved her fully remote situation because he was familiar with her name. PDX has a biweekly meeting among development groups where individuals can volunteer to present their team's work. White said, "There's a lot of opportunities to volunteer for visible training or leading a meeting." She's tried to do that as much as she can, because the more her name is said in upper management meetings the better—they won't ever have to make a hard case for additional compensation when your name comes up.

One of the reasons she's especially proactive is because there tends to be a wage gap in the technology industry. White insisted that going on Glassdoor and doing research is really important.

"Knowing what you're worth and what value you bring to a company is important in any company or industry," she said.

Now, White only wonders if she's too comfortable. She's "getting recruiting calls all the time" from big names in the technology industry like Google and Apple. Those same qualities that allowed her to work remotely in the first place are now allowing her to succeed directly from her home office and have other employers recruiting her to come work for them.

CHAPTER 9

FIND REMOTE WORK

"Quit sooner because the rest of your life is waiting."

That's the advice of Alex Fasulo, a twenty-five-year-old free-lance writer who lives in Brooklyn, N.Y., works remotely, and makes six figures. She's been freelancing full-time since 2015, and prior to that, she had never worked remotely before. As she told her story on the LenJones Party of 2 podcast in September 2018, Fasulo laid out how her unique career path transpired.[30] For nearly four years, she's been grinding, and her hard work is paying off. She's now making $300,000

---

30 Lenhart, Ian. "How this 25-year-old made $150,000 in 6 months off of Fiverr." *Len Jones Party of 2*. https://soundcloud.com/user-895506531/11-how-this-25-year-old-freelancer-made-150000-in-6-months-off-fiverr (June 17, 2019).

working remotely on Fiverr and operating a social media management company.

"Yeah, no I mean you're making it sound all glamorous. No, this year's been nuts because I'm finally reaping the benefits of grinding very hard at the freelance lifestyle for over three years. It's surreal but I won't say it's not deserved," she said of where she is now.

Fiverr, pronounced "five-er," is the world's largest freelance platform. It allows freelancers to market themselves in a variety of categories to entrepreneurs who can hire them at a day-to-day price via the internet. Fasulo works in the "writing & translation" section of the website, but it also includes graphics/design, digital marketing, video/animation, music/audio, programming/tech, business, and fun/lifestyle.

Fiverr is where Fasulo ended up, but that's not where she started. She's twenty-five, which means she really is only a few years out of college. This is what makes her early success all the more interesting. Originally from Albany, she attended State University of New York College at Geneseo in Rochester, N.Y., and graduated a year early.

"Immediately after graduating college, I went to go work back in Albany because that's just, you know, what I knew. And I had always been kind of interested in politics—that type of thing—which I'm not going to get into, but I went to school for political science, so naturally I thought I'd go work at the New York State Assembly, which was great. And I actually made the best friends of my life there, and I talk to all of them pretty much every single day still. But after a year and a half or so, I just felt like—it's so cliche—but I just felt like I had more to give, and I wasn't able to give it there. It didn't really make sense. I was only twenty-two. I graduated a year early so I was only twenty-two at the time I was still, like, 'I don't even know [what I'm] doing, but something tells me that I can do more than this,' and I just kind of listened to that tug."

Fasulo was happy where she was but she felt that pull to do more. She was young, she was smart, and she wanted to see if she could make the "New York City jump." Her original job working as a press coordinator at the New York State Assembly had come about because she had done a summer internship there while she was in college. The next one didn't come as easily. Fasulo says she had to apply to around three hundred places before someone would finally give her an interview at a public relations firm. When she finally moved to New York City and started working at her new job, it wasn't at all what she imagined.

"I absolutely hated this PR firm I was working at," she said without hesitation, "I am not someone who cries, and I do not cry in public. I am a very type A, show-no-weakness type of person, and I was sobbing on my keyboard everyday."

Fasulo says that she even texted her mom one day, "I feel like I'm a fairy in a cage and they're plucking my wings off of me." Her new job was less public relations and more secretarial work, which Fasulo said just wasn't up her alley. She now knows, "I have to do something creative every day. I now know this or I feel like I'm dying."

In any case, Fasulo lasted around four weeks at her new PR job before she quit. She emailed in her resignation because she couldn't stand going to work. She was tired of hating her job. She was also afraid that now that she had quit, she was going to have to move back home to Albany, and she was going to get made fun of for having failed.

That night, when she went home, Fasulo changed her life forever by logging back onto her Fiverr account, something she had set up only about a year beforehand at her mom's suggestion.

"She said, 'Hey, check out this site. You can maybe make a little side cash at your job or whatever.' So, I had one gig, that's what they're called on Fiverr, which is a service you offer. I offered editing for $5—like no money for a couple months—for like half a year. I didn't take it very seriously at all. I was making like $35 a month from it. But I thought it was cool because I had a salary, so I was like 'Oh I can buy, like, a new pair of jeans from this side money, this is sick.' But I didn't know much about Fiverr. I didn't know really what it could do for me until that, like, moment came where it was like do or die."

While she had this Fiverr account for a year, Fasulo had never ever needed it to make ends meet. Now, she really needed it. She wasn't going to be able to pay rent without the job that she quit, so she put up some new gigs and woke up to what most would call "overnight success."

"It happened pretty quickly that night. It was like December 7. I honestly remember the day."

December 7, 2015, was the day that Fasulo began to think that there might be something to this freelancing, working remotely game. She acknowledged that her first job at the New York State Assembly as a press coordinator really set her up to be successful.

"I definitely couldn't be doing what I'm doing today not having worked that job first, to be honest, because I worked as a Press Coordinator, which is essentially what I'm doing now today privately for businesses instead of politicians. They taught me press releases, Facebook posts, everything I now sell today. So, I owe my head start to them for sure."

Yet, after that experience, she was able to leverage what she knew to be successful online right from the apartment where she was paying rent (and the Starbucks around the corner). Fasulo says it was in February 2016 that she made her first full $100. That's when she felt like celebrating and said, "I wanna go out to dinner, I made $100 from my laptop."

In March 2016, the orders started coming in so quickly that she could hardly handle the demand. Her first year, she made around $40,000, which now seems like a drop in the bucket compared to what she is making. Still, her hustling allowed her to stay in her Brooklyn apartment while making cash from her laptop.

It's not all fun and games though. Fasulo really was hustling. "You have no idea what I did for no money for so long," she said.

Part of the game that Fiverr freelancers play is with reviews. As Fasulo says, "It's all about reviews." When a seller is hired by a buyer on the platform, both parties have the opportunity to rate the interaction. For sellers, this matters tremendously as buyers will default to individuals with 5-star reviews. For Fasulo, who boasts almost 4,000 5-star reviews, it's no wonder buyers look to her when they need a project done quickly and professionally.

She also said, "I have an advantage now having been with them for almost four years." When you have a 5-star average that's so deep, not even "cranky" people can mess with that type of average. A buyer who gives you an undeserved one-star review won't impact your overall averages because of the sheer number of positive ones.

In April 2017, Fiverr selected Fasulo for a more elite portal they were launching: Fiverr Pro. Pro intended to cherry-pick the top sellers and showcase these professionals on their own platform. Fasulo was told that she was selected for the platform only when she arrived at the warehouse in Brooklyn where Fiverr was shooting the commercial for Pro. She couldn't comprehend how her life was going to change.

Fiverr Pro means that Fasulo can now charge more for her services since her new clientele is seeking vetted talent for large quantities of orders. Her business has expanded immensely, and while Fasulo is still learning, she's getting to the point where she needs to grow her business by hiring employees. She says she spends anywhere from three to four hours a day just responding to customer service inquiries. Hiring someone to help her with these might speed up business, but she said she's still figuring out the best way to do so. She said, "Yeah, so I'm at a point that I want to scale, but I would never give my Fiverr password to anyone but my mom or my sister because it's like one password between nothing and like hundreds of thousands of dollars. So yes, in theory, I would love to have someone like that helping me to organize things like that, but for right now I just couldn't open up the account to someone like that. That would make me lose even more sleep, you know?"

She's not opposed to working with someone, and it might even be someone remotely, she's just still coming to understand how it would work best for her as a remote worker herself.

Fasulo said, "I've been thinking more about people that I know and having someone that I could possibly see in person every so often and use Slack with. I'm a fan of Slack, that messaging platform. Something that I could still deliver all the initial projects [through] because I don't want anyone going into any of my accounts—I just don't."

That's the thing about hitting $300,000 at twenty-five years old, you're still learning. Fasulo said she "knows the natural next step is scaling." It's just difficult in her specific industry. "Specifically this niche that I'm in is difficult," she said, "I make the money I make because of the written content I produce, which is not easy to come by today."

She knows that she'll need to work with whomever she might hire in the future to get them up to the speed she's at because she didn't start out at this speed. "When I first started doing it back in that winter, I was freaking out because I couldn't handle all the orders I was getting," Fasulo said, "I didn't have the discipline for this. I didn't know how to write words as fast as I know how to write them today, so it's definitely been a four-year-coming thing. So, the pace that I write now is superhuman, but I don't think that I was born superhuman."

That's one big takeaway of making any remote work dream possible. There's no doubt that Fasulo is superb at what she does, but she's also always aspiring to be better. When she doubled her income from $40,000 to $80,000, there was no stopping there. Her next goal was $100,000. Now, she's tripled that. There are seven-figure Fiverr professionals out there, and there's still somewhere to go. What her story tells us is that it is possible to use the skills you have, to find something that you love to do, and to do it right from where you want to do it.

Right now, that place for Fasulo is Brooklyn, N.Y. In starting out on her Fiverr path, Fasulo was truly part of the "digital nomad" era of Millennials who are no longer tied to their desks. She doesn't report to an office, she goes to the gym in the middle of the day, and she abides by her own schedule... but Fasulo says that does mean having a schedule.

"I'm still such a scheduled type of person, so it's like, even though I can make my schedule, I still keep the same one every single day, and that is that I immediately get to work when I wake up. I'm not like an open newspaper/coffee, I'm like let's go, let's go because otherwise the work piles up. I sit in my pajamas, working, head down from like 7 a.m. 'til noon like, 'do not talk to me,'" she said, "And then at noon, I go to the gym because I need to move at that point, I feel gross. I go to the gym, make lunch, take a shower, and then I try to not look terrible for the rest of the day. By like 3 p.m."

While she does work a normal amount of hours in a day, Fiverr's online platform allowed Fasulo to work just about anywhere with internet access. Now, she cranks out pieces in the quiet of her swanky new Brooklyn Heights apartment, but she used to do it in the Starbucks around the corner from her apartment in the Bushwick neighborhood of Brooklyn. Her original gig, editing, had mostly foreign clients who needed help with their English, and she has roughly thirty messages coming in overnight every night because Fiverr operates in every time zone across the globe. If Fiverr isn't dependent on a location, would Fasulo ever consider the truly nomadic life?

"Sometimes I want to just get up and go travel for three months. But then the other part of me likes to still have a routine and be here in the city and a lot of what I have now is because I've hung around New York City for a few years. I also don't like to travel alone and I don't really know anyone who is in the position I'm in so I'm always trying to force people to come with me."

Her early success has made it nearly impossible for her peers to keep up with her lifestyle, but she knows people, [and writing] is what makes her happy. "My happiness comes from people," she said, "I'm a very strong family person and my sister's here in the city. I don't have a desire to just get up and go somewhere for a year and leave everyone behind."

That said, Fasulo knows that working remotely can be something that provides experiences beyond any others if you capitalize on them at the right moment. "I also at the same time do recognize my unique situation and my age and one day when you have kids you can't do this anymore, so I definitely—before I'm thirty—I want to at least do a cross country, multi-month, totally immersive thing. I want to do a 'backpack Europe thing' and go to as many other places before then as I can. Next stop is New Orleans for Halloween."

Fasulo has built her career doing what she loves and she recommends everyone do the same. "Figure out what your passion is—what you love to do—because it is going to be a bumpy and wild ride. And it's going to require so much attention and dedication and everything you have, that at least pick something that you love if you're going to do it," she said.

"For me, I've always loved writing. You need to at least like what you're doing. Don't just chase a buck, do what you love to do. What's that quote? 'Do what you love to do and you'll never work a day in your life.' It's true."

* * *

Fasulo's freelancing style of remote work might not be for you, but her approach to finding something that works for her can be. She found something that she was good at and ran with it, and Caplan did the same. Both of these individuals married their desire for freedom with their desire to work in a way that was fulfilling to them. **You can do it too.**

After getting this far in this book, you might be wondering, "Okay, maybe I can, but **how do I find a remote work opportunity?**"

Perhaps you work in retail or healthcare, or perhaps like Samara Wenten, who worked as an educator in a classroom, you're in a part of your industry that can't possibly be remote, though there may be a job in an industry out there that can fit your remote desires.

Sometimes, starting to look for something new is the hardest part of the entire process, so here's a starting point.[31]

---

31   Caplan, Greg. "Top 4 Ways to Get a Remote Job." Remote Year. https:// remoteyear.com/blog/top-4-ways-to-get-a-remote-job (June 17, 2019).

* * *

STEP #1: THINK ABOUT YOUR CURRENT JOB

Of course, this is the first go-to because it's the job you already have. It's the one that you know, and the one where your employer knows you. You have a reputation at this job (and hopefully a good one at that). If you're in a good spot with your position and you like it, then there's no reason not to pitch remote work to your employer. Use the playbook in Chapter 9 and go for it.

Remember, the worst thing that happens is that your boss says, "No." If this happens, you can go on to Step #2, but it's still worth asking because transitioning a role you already know to a remote setting is often easier than trying to learn an entirely new role while also getting the hang of being a remote employee.

STEP #2: THINK ABOUT YOUR INDUSTRY

Now, this shouldn't discourage anyone since we've heard HR gurus like Hilliary Turnipseed say that you can do most jobs from anywhere, though certain industries may be particularly inclined to go on the road or to a home office. Perhaps you're already in an industry that rocks for remote work, and you can use this to your advantage. These include jobs in the following industries:[32]

- Technology
- Marketing
- Customer Success
- UX and Graphic Design
- Human Resources
- And more!

Don't get discouraged. If the field or industry that you're interested in isn't on this list, it doesn't mean that you're doomed to a 9-to-5 office job forever. It just means you may have to get creative in how you become remote. Alex Fasulo didn't become remote via the PR firm she hated working for, but created her own opportunity through a freelance platform using the skills she had learned in a previous workplace.

Greg Caplan has also highlighted that it's crucial to reflect on how your job could be done differently today—in an ever-advancing technological world—even if you don't believe it could be remote. Remember, just because your job isn't labeled "remote" now doesn't mean that it doesn't have that potential. In fact, he says, "if you could do 80 percent or more of your daily tasks solely from a phone or computer,

---

32   "7 Jobs You Can Do From Anywhere." Remote Year. https://remot-eyear.com/blog/jobs-you-can-do-from-anywhere (June 17, 2019.)

you could work remotely." Thinking about how your industry and position works on a daily basis, even if no one else is, could be a game changer in how you come to maximize your own productivity.

STEP #3: THINK ABOUT YOUR LOCATION

This might be the wildest way that you launch yourself into working remotely, but remote workers are becoming more and more desirable, and guess what? Cities are now paying you and your laptop to move locations and work remotely. Yes, for real.

In November 2018, CBS reported that a Tulsa, Okla., billionaire was offering $10,000 and a co-working space to *each* remote worker who would relocate to Tulsa to work remotely.[33] While this might sound absurd, the offer to move to a certain state isn't unique to Oklahoma. Vermont has also released similar tax and cash incentives. So, if you're up for relocating (which admittedly isn't for everyone) and want to work remotely, keep an eye out for these types of opportunities. It's becoming a new and innovative way for companies

---

33 Smith, Kate. "Tulsa, Oklahoma, will pay you $10,000 to move there. But there's a catch." CBS News. https://www.cbsnews.com/news/tulsa-oklahoma-will-pay-you-10000-to-move-there-but-theres-a-catch/ (June 17, 2019).

to attract talented workers, and it's working. Thousands of applicants have already applied.

STEP #4: THINK ABOUT YOUR NETWORK

Doesn't everything start with the network? LinkedIn estimates that around 80 percent of individuals find jobs through people that they already know (I know because I read this in the vast majority of emails that they send me). Yet, the sentiment holds true. Your network is vast, and the odds are likely that you know someone who works remotely either part or full-time because of how common it's becoming.

While it's probably not your best bet to message someone you only "just know" on LinkedIn to ask about working remotely, you can take advantage of your connections and any connections that your connections have. It's okay to ask for help on your journey toward maximizing your own productivity.

STEP #5: THINK ABOUT A NEW JOB

Admittedly, this isn't the preferred route. Again, the job you have is the one you want to go remote with, but if you're unhappy, you're looking for a change, your pitch just didn't go as planned, or Steps #2-4 didn't result in anything promising, here you are. The cold job search is scary and probably not a position you want to be in. If you're going to search for a remote job, following Caplan's steps for how to do it "right."

1. Keep the passion you have for your work. One of the worst mistakes you can make when cold applying is simply applying because a job is remote. It should still be a position you're interested in because of the industry and role. Once you've found a position that stands out to you, reach out to the hiring manager.

2. Rather than limiting yourself to exclusively remote positions, find positions that fit well with your experience and industry desires AND can also fit well with being remote. Remember the checklist in Chapter 2? Go back and use that as a reference. You can always pitch a flexible work arrangement as a necessity for you to accept the job once you're at the negotiation stage. You now have the tools to make your case.

3. Follow companies that are fully-distributed and that you know have remote work arrangements. This will require a bit of homework, but once you establish a list and do a bit of research, you'll be able to keep an eye out for any of the jobs that they're releasing. Reach out to a hiring manager or any contacts you may have in your network at these companies for an informational interview.

* * *

While finding or pitching remote work may seem like a daunting task, putting your work needs and productivity at the forefront of your professional career is essential to finding success. In his time in the remote work space, Caplan has observed that remote workers are often the top performers in their fields. If they weren't, then they wouldn't be in a position to take their work with them wherever they are most productive. Stand by your gut if this type of work is for you, and like Fasulo says, you'll never work a day in your life.

CHAPTER 10

REMOTE WORK: A CASE STUDY

In Chapter 5, you heard Greg Caplan talk about a big idea he had and why he had it. He wanted to travel the world and he wanted to do it by working remotely, but he didn't just believe that remote work was an alternative work arrangement. For Caplan, working remotely is quickly becoming a talent acquisition strategy. Caplan believes that remote work will become a part of that "suite of benefits" that entices workers to take some jobs over others or work with a certain company over the next.

Yet, remote work is not immune from the workplace debate. In fact, we've already seen two large companies, Yahoo and IBM, publicly criticized for their ineffective remote work policies. This begs the question: Is remote work effective? Will it continue to work in current workplaces, or is work only meant for an office?

Remote work may sound fabulous on paper...until you try it and find out that your own personal productivity cannot possibly thrive in that environment. Remote work in real life is different than it is on paper. Yahoo's "remote work ban" illustrates this. This chapter will take a closer look at the Yahoo case study and how winning remotely requires modern technology that has boomed in the last five years as well as management tactics that have been discussed in the preceding chapters.

THE REMOTE WORK BAN

In 2013, Yahoo's then-CEO Marissa Mayer became well-known for "banning" remote work. At the time, this policy made headlines across the United States and sparked "a remote work debate." It also came near the time that IBM pulled nearly all of their employees back into their offices for a different set of reasons. As it became a newsworthy topic, Yahoo's remote work policy (at least on paper) appeared to be ammunition for employers around the world to say, "See? It didn't work."

Yet, that's not quite the case. While Yahoo might have tested the waters and largely recalled their employees, Mayer clarified exactly why Yahoo did so at the time in an interview with Steven Levy on WIRED, and it didn't sound like remote work wouldn't work forever.[34] Rather, Yahoo couldn't make it work then, and there were specific reasons why.

"Well, I mean, I think that I really didn't mean for it to become an industry narrative in terms of whether or not people could actually successfully work from home. We were saying that it's not right for us right now," Mayer said.

An issue that Mayer cited as one of the primary obstacles for Yahoo's remote work policy was the distribution of their teams. Having to coordinate meetings with individuals who were working all over the country or telecommuting from home was creating what Mayer described as "drag." In other words, it was lowering productivity. To fix it, Yahoo decided to bring all of their workers back into the office.

"As a general principle—obviously there are exceptions, and we made a lot of exceptions—you know, we want people in the office. I think that overall it was actually really well-received inside the company, and it was the right thing for us right now."

---

34 "Marissa Mayer Responds to Yahoo Work-from-Home Criticism." YouTube. https://www.youtube.com/watch?v=SJKdGLKQEtU (June 17, 2019).

Now, while this may be true that Yahoo didn't have the infrastructure to handle remote workers right now, it doesn't mean that remote workers are the core of the issue. The support for remote work just has to exist before it can be reimplemented. We know that working remotely is an emerging trend, in part, because of two factors. One is because of the technology that now exists. The second is because of the workplace culture that is growing to support it, partially because of said technology.

HOW TECHNOLOGY HAS CHANGED REMOTE WORK

With the technology that now connects businesses across the globe—think the Cloud, Slack, Zoom, and sharing platforms like Google Drive—it has become that much easier to work from home. There's no need to get up and walk something over to your coworker's desk. You can just as easily tag them or send them a chat message to connect with them instantly. In many ways, technology has created more efficient ways than ever for workplaces to communicate. While some of these platforms may have existed back in 2013, they weren't as integrated into workplace settings in the same way. These platforms have to infiltrate the workspace user by user, and if they're not well-integrated then they won't be well-utilized.

Had Yahoo been able to slowly move back toward working remotely in the years to come, they likely would have had greater success utilizing the newly available technology. Now, coordination of meetings and working with a dispersed team can be easily compensated for with both Zoom and Slack. Companies around the country and globe are doing this everyday. Clear communication just has to exist in order for it to occur.

The disconnect within their distributed teams likely doesn't indicate the inability of remote work to function in a workplace, but may instead suggest either the misuse of available resources or the wrong individuals utilizing the avenue of remote work. Remote work isn't for everyone either, which is why companies should be wary of mandating it. Although it can be incredibly advantageous, employees need to know how to be productive in their space, and some individuals aren't capable of it in the same way that others are, which may lower productivity for some workers. Allowing individuals to work how they work best is incredibly beneficial to companies and their productivity.

Now, unfortunately, this theory can't be tested as Yahoo was officially bought out by Verizon in the summer of 2017. Yet, the failures of Yahoo and how it could have improved are vital in understanding how to move forward in the remote work conversation. It is easy to look at a massive company like Yahoo and say, "Well, if it didn't work for them, then it must not work at all, right?" Wrong. The world and workspace are changing concurrently, and that's what is most essential to keep in mind.

The second reason that Mayer cites is the lack of collaboration that occurs when individuals are not in the office. She says that individuals are much more likely to be innovative when they are in an office space, and that is what Yahoo needed at the time.

"During normal business hours, generally, we want people to be there collaborating with their teams because I do ascribe to the theory that basically shows that people are in fact more productive when they work alone, but not surprisingly, they are more collaborative and inventive when they work together," Mayer said.

As an example, Mayer pointed to how the Yahoo weather app was created. She says it was largely the result of two individuals running into each other in the office. "You needed someone from Flickr to say, 'Hey I've got these geotagged photos and I know where these photos were taken, and we can probably detect whether or not they're spaces in them or whether they're a scene,' running into someone from Weather and saying, 'Could we make our app more beautiful?' I kind of call it the Reese's peanut butter effect. What happens when we combine these things?"

Mayer's point is well-taken in some ways. The office is meant to be a collaborative space. It's meant to bring individuals together and enable them to work together on various projects to help make the company more successful. Where this becomes a problem is when the office space inhibits people from being productive. While Yahoo surely needed to be collaborative, it likely needed to be productive even more. So, the key question is, how do you make a workspace both productive and collaborative? These are the two fundamental elements that Yahoo seemed to lack and it's why they called back all their workers from their widely-utilized remote policy.

That said, it's interesting to look at the functions that now allow remote collaboration. For example, co-working spaces such as WeWork or break out rooms like Zoom offer the ability for workers (either working from home, in the same city, or entirely remotely) to come together for brainstorming sessions.

Would you get the same result you might from someone just casually bumping into someone else in the office? No, probably not. Yet, saying that there aren't tools or platforms for remote collaboration out there just isn't true. The fact is that remote work and collaboration need to work a bit differently, and people need to be on top of it. If the problem Yahoo was having was that there was "drag" because people weren't answering meeting invites at the right time, the problem is with the employee.

Overall, Mayer's decision to place a "ban" on remote work doesn't indicate that remote work can't be a way that business functions, or rather, functions well. There were a number of factors that contributed to its "failure" prior to 2013, when Mayer made the decision to pull everyone back in. Some of these factors are no longer relevant because we've developed technology to circumvent the issues. Other factors are long-term issues that need to be handled based on the personnel you're working with.

* * *

It's important to remember that working remotely takes both an effective employer and an effective employee in the arrangement. However, it's just as important to bear in mind that remote work isn't for everyone. If you think it's for you, then you need to make sure you have the tools, team, and communication skills to do your work effectively and efficiently. Once you do, you can do it from anywhere in the world with nothing holding you back.

CONCLUSION

———

I started this book with a story about how I had created a remote "side hustle" for myself one day while sitting idly in class. Over the last nine months—during the same period that I've written this book—a "side hustle" that I once planned to use for beer money has grown into a rent-paying, grocery-paying income. I kickstarted this whole journey (the book and working remotely) by reading Alex Fasulo's story, and the whole thing has been both more rewarding and more challenging than I ever could have imagined.

My experience, even from a freelancing perspective, has allowed me to come to terms with what remote workers handle every single day. From simple and frustrating Wi-Fi issues to the larger misconceptions of what remote work means as a work style.

In fact, I recently read the following quote, "This is the one big problem with working remotely: no one believes you have a job at all."

And it hit me. This couldn't be more true. For others and for myself. It had been a sentiment that I heard expressed in my interviews with people and one I have felt myself. While remote workers face all kinds of challenges with their blended teams, management, lack of Wi-Fi, and remote workspaces, perhaps their largest challenge of all was convincing others that their work is real and valuable.

Based on my research, on what I had read, and those I have talked to, it always seemed like you have to do just a little bit more and go just a bit "above and beyond" to hit a bar that's held so high. If anything, a remote worker's work often has to be *more real* and *more valuable* than average because they're automatically perceived as doing less. The truly coveted jobs in this world are the ones that make you appear to work less than average (even if that's not always the case). They're the ones that provide the most flexibility and that maximize your productivity, so that you can make your work-life balance what it needs to be.

The stories in this book indicate that there's a world of professionals out there willing to take a risk to make their jobs and lives better through a different style of work. They work long hours and work through all the connectivity and communication challenges that accompany their remote setting, and they still get hit with these types of branded misconceptions. And while this might not apply to the vast majority of modern professionals today, learning to make a professional environment work for you isn't something invalid, or something that you should need to justify.

Nine months ago, I couldn't possibly imagine my life behind a desk or in a 9-to-5 format. And I still can't. The words on these pages haven't just been written in the quaint D.C. neighborhood where I recently graduated from college. They've been written in Costa Rica, New Zealand, Australia, and Indonesia. They've been written in airports, on airplanes, and in coffee shops. They serve as a reminder that connectivity and productivity can indeed be anywhere if you make it so.

If you're ready for your own journey into remote work, don't hesitate to get started. If you're an employer, implement a flexible work policy at your company. Coach your management on how to facilitate blended work and implement onboarding and tools that support remote workers. In the day and age of digital nomads, this type of benefit only makes you more attractive as a company.

If you're an employee, do just as Alex Fasulo says and, "Quit sooner, because the rest of your life is waiting." Use the perspectives and the stories in this book to maximize your journey and pitch remote work to your employer. There are others out there who have done exactly what you hope to do. Learn from and lean on their experiences.

Remember, working remotely might not be for everyone, but it certainly could be for you.

www.ingramcontent.com/pod-product-compliance
Lightning Source LLC
Chambersburg PA
CBHW071523180526
45171CB00002B/364